GREAT
PIONEER
PROJECTS

YOU CAN BUILD YOURSELF

RACHEL DICKINSON

nomad press

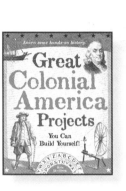

Nomad Press
A division of Nomad Communications
10 9 8 7 6 5 4 3 2 1
Copyright © 2007 by Nomad Press
All rights reserved.

ISBN: 0-9785037-6-7
978-0-9785037-6-5
Questions regarding the ordering of this book should be addressed to
Independent Publishers Group
814 N. Franklin St., Chicago, IL 60610
www.ipgbook.com

Nomad Press
2456 Christian St., White River Junction, VT 05001
www.nomadpress.net

Image Credits

Cover photo of train by Börries Burkhardt; prospector, p.2 / wagon train, p.28: **Used by permission, Utah State Historical Society, all rights reserved**; Louisiana Purchase, p.5/Buffalo Bill, p.6/Lewis and Clark, p.7/Clark field notes, p.8/Lewis, p.8/Clark, p.9/Mexican War, p.18/Manifest Destiny (George A. Crofutt, artist), p.19/Laura Ingalls Wilder, p.20/Oklahoma Land Rush (McClenny Family Picture Album), p.21/Sutter's mine, p.22/Bodie, CA, p.22/John Sutter, p.23/Deadwood, p.24/Custer, p.24/Joseph Smith, p.48: **from Wikipedia**; panning for gold, p.21/first sod home, p.67/log cabin, p.68/log cabin, p.68/teams plowing, p.74/school, p.84/branding cattle, p.101: **from the Library of Congress**; emmigrant's guide, p.42/Fort Hall, p.46/ Whitmans, p.46/log cabin, p.71: **from the National Park Service**; laying tracks, p.61/golden spike ceremony, p.62/turning sod, p.65: from the U.S. National Archives (USNA); Levis, p.25: courtesy of PatentMuseum.com; wagon train, p.26: http://www.sonofthesouth.net/; soddie, p.66: from National Agriculture Library; quilting bee, p.74: courtesy of Middlesex Historical Society, from *Middlesex in the Making: History and Memories of a Small Vermont Town*, by Sarah Seidman and Patty Wiley; pottery, p.82: courtesy of Dargate Auction Galleries LLC / www.dargate.com; girl spinning, p.83: courtesy of Alden House Historic Site; cowboy, p.102: courtesy of Horse Prairie Ranch, Dillon, Montana; turkey, p.94: Pennsylvania Game Commission, photo by Joe Kosack; longhorn, p.103: courtesy of Butler Texas Longhorn.

CONTENTS

TIMELINE of THE PIONEERS

1803: President Thomas Jefferson purchases the Louisiana Territory from France for $15 million. This extends the United States borders from the Mississippi River to the Rocky Mountains.

1804: Meriwether Lewis and William Clark and the Corps of Discovery head out to explore the Louisiana Territory.

1806: Lewis and Clark return after reaching the Pacific Ocean.

1810: The U.S. annexes West Florida from Spain that includes parts of modern-day Alabama, Louisiana, and Mississippi.

1819: The U.S. annexes East Florida, which makes up present day Florida.

1830: Congress passes the Indian Removal Act, giving President Andrew Jackson the power to remove Native Americans from the east to lands west of the Mississippi River.

1834: The Indian Territory is established in what is now Oklahoma. This is to serve as home for Native Americans who are displaced by white settlers.

1836: Defeat at the Alamo. Later the same year the Republic of Texas wins independence from Mexico.

1842: John C. Fremont makes accurate maps of the West.

1843: The first wagon train settlers from the East travel west along the Oregon Trail in the Great Migration.

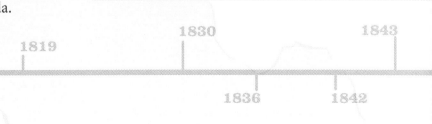

1803	1806	1819		1830	1843
1804	1810			1836	1842

1844: The U.S. signs a treaty with the Republic of Texas to annex an area that includes Texas and parts of what are now Colorado, New Mexico, and Oklahoma.

1845: The U.S. annexes Texas. John L. O'Sullivan coins the term Manifest Destiny.

1846: The Mormons begin leaving Nauvoo, Illinois, to head west to their new home near the Great Salt Lake. Beginning of the Mexican-American War.

1848: Gold is discovered at Sutter's mill in California. The U.S. gains what is now California, Nevada, Utah, and parts of Colorado, New Mexico, Arizona, and Wyoming as a result of the end of the Mexican-American War. The US also annexes the Oregon Territory containing what is now Idaho, Oregon, Washington, and parts of Montana and Wyoming.

1853: For $10 million, the U.S. buys what is today part of Arizona and New Mexico in the Gadsden Purchase.

1860: The Pony Express operates a speedy delivery service in the west. Young men and fast horses deliver the mail in breakneck speed covering sometimes as much as 250 miles per day. This mail service lasts about 18 months until the telegraph puts them out of business.

1861: Telegraph line is completed between San Francisco and St. Louis, effectively making the Pony Express obsolete.

1862: Congress passes the Homestead Act, which encourages settlers to move west. Many settle on the Great Plains, on lands reserved for Native Americans.

1867: The U.S. purchases the Alaska Territory from Russia for $7.2 million.

1869: The rails of the Central Pacific and Union Pacific railroads meet at Promontory Point near Ogden, Utah, inaugurating cross-country train travel.

1872: Yellowstone National Park is established as the nation's first national park.

1874: Barbed wire is patented, a small invention that will change the look of the Great Plains.

1876: George Custer is defeated at the Battle of Little Bighorn.

1883: The buffalo on the Great Plains are almost completely exterminated—only 200 remain.

1889: A huge portion of Indian Territory is opened for white homesteaders leading to the Oklahoma Land Rush.

1890: The U.S. Census Bureau declares the West settled and the frontier "closed."

1844 1848 1860 1867 1872 1876 1889

1846 1853 1862 1869 1874 1883 1890
1845 1861

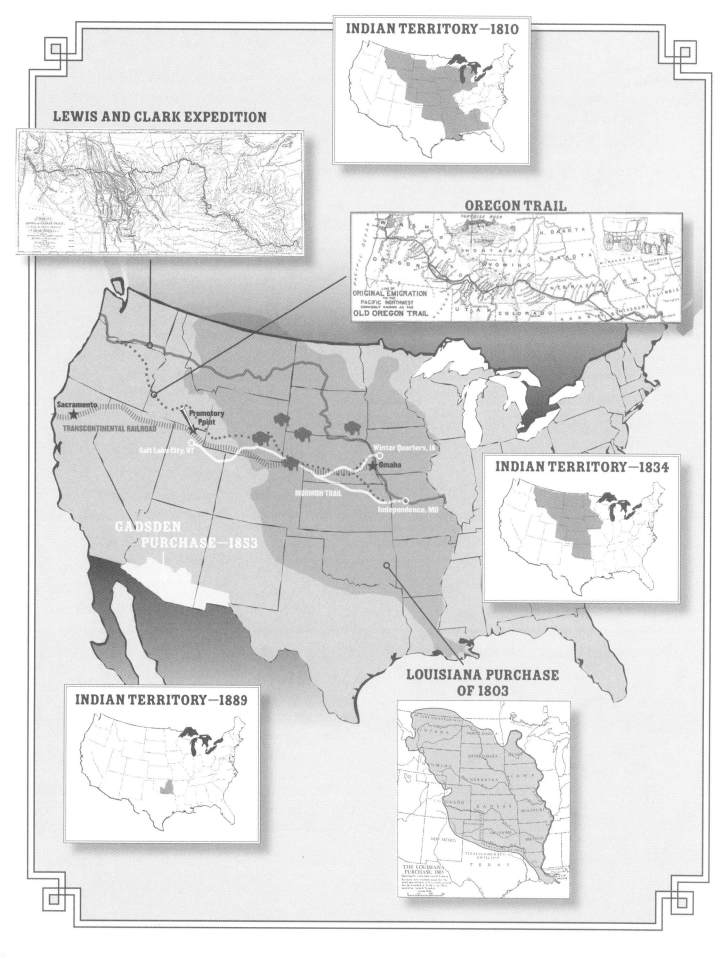

INDIAN TERRITORY—1810

LEWIS AND CLARK EXPEDITION

OREGON TRAIL

ORIGINAL EMIGRATION
TO THE
PACIFIC NORTHWEST
COMMONLY KNOWN AS THE
OLD OREGON TRAIL

Sacramento

TRANSCONTINENTAL RAILROAD

Promotory
Point

Salt Lake City, UT

Winter Quarters, IA

Omaha

MORMON TRAIL

Independence, MO

INDIAN TERRITORY—1834

**GADSDEN
PURCHASE—1853**

INDIAN TERRITORY—1889

**LOUISIANA PURCHASE
OF 1803**

THE LOUISIANA
PURCHASE, 1803

INTRODUCTION

PIONEER IS SOMEONE WHO DOES SOMETHING FIRST or who leads in developing something new. For example, Jonas Salk was a **pioneer** in medicine because he was the first to create the polio vaccine. Jackie Robinson was a pioneer in baseball because he was the first African-American player to play in the major leagues. What do we call the first Americans who bravely traveled west into uncharted territory? That's right, American pioneers.

American pioneers came from all walks of life—farmers, shopkeepers, businessmen, factory workers, women, children, and **immigrants**—but they all shared a common vision. They yearned for a better life and a piece of land they could call their own. They were willing to give up all of their possessions to make this happen. While most of them did not become famous, they were all very brave. Pioneer families from all over the East and Midwest endured the hardships of the trail as they traveled thousands of miles on foot in search of a new home.

In **Great Pioneer Projects You Can Build Yourself** you'll learn about the history of the American West and the pioneers who traveled there. You'll see how brave they had to be to leave their family, friends, and homes behind to embark on these journeys into the unknown. And you'll read about how difficult the pioneers' lives were while on the trail and once they settled in the **frontier**. These were the days before video games, cell phones, gas-powered tools and machines, and cars—and, remember, there wasn't even any indoor plumbing. On top of all that, when these pioneers reached the end of the trail they had to build a home and figure out how to survive on the edge of the frontier. Because there were no stores to buy food, clothing, or building materials, they had to learn how to make everything they needed from scratch and by hand.

As you read about all the challenges the pioneers faced you'll be amazed at the obstacles they overcame. As you take part in the activities you'll get to experience some of these challenges yourself. Among other things, you'll map the western territories, sew your own pouches and clothes, make your own food and journal, and even build your own log cabin and sod house. So get ready to step back in time, head out on the trail, and **Build It Yourself!**

HOW IT ALL BEGAN

OR MANY PEOPLE, THE WORD "FRONTIER" BRINGS TO mind images of the Wild West. Maybe the word makes you think of cowboys and Indians, or a stagecoach pulled by a team of horses, kicking up a cloud of dust in a vast dry landscape. Or maybe the word paints a scene of a frontier town with horses tied to a hitching post in front of a saloon with swinging doors. Some who hear the word "frontier" see a miner with a long beard and a hat panning for gold in a creek, while others imagine a long train of covered wagons, loaded with pioneers and all their belongings.

The frontier is the edge of what is known—the farthest point of a civilization or settlement—and throughout much of America's history that meant the frontier was to the west. Not long after Europeans settled along the East Coast, some settlers began to move west, inland, in search of land, natural resources like water, and animals to hunt. As more Europeans came to the New World to start a new life, and as the population of the colonies began to grow, the desire to explore the West increased. Colonists wanted to claim a piece of the wilderness before someone else did—and they didn't want to settle for leftovers. They wanted good fertile land that could be farmed and hunted.

Movement West

After the colonists won the Revolutionary War and gained their freedom from England, the government and the country as a whole focused on developing the West. The government figured that if people moved west and farmed and improved the land, it would not only be profitable for the individuals who moved there, but for the entire country. With this belief in mind, America's third president, Thomas Jefferson, bought a big chunk of land from France in 1803. It reached beyond the Mississippi River into the West. This was called the Louisiana Purchase. A year later, President Jefferson asked Meriwether Lewis and William Clark to explore the territory from the Missouri River to the Columbia River (in present-day Oregon). Lewis and Clark's expedition, called the Corps of Discovery, was very successful. They brought back complete reports of their findings, as well as maps of the Northwest Territory that inspired and paved the way for other American pioneers to follow in their footsteps.

Throughout the course of the nineteenth century great changes took place in America as pioneers moved west. Before the Louisiana Purchase most of the United States settlements were along the East Coast. The only Americans (or Europeans) who lived inland then were mountain men and trappers. But in the early 1800s this began to change. Floods of **emigrants** streamed into the frontier—first by wagon train and later by sea and railroad—and carved homesteads, ranches, and communities out of undeveloped forestland and **prairie**. Most people were lured to the West by the promise of land, the hope of finding gold, or the idea of a place where they could practice their religion without **persecution**. And many people developed these expectations when they saw posters known as broadsides, advertisements in newspapers, or letters from family and friends who had already made the journey. All of these sources portrayed the West as a paradise where fertile land and natural resources like gold were plentiful.

As more and more pioneers were persuaded to hit the trail, the frontier line moved farther west, and the North American landscape west of the Mississippi River began to change. Cattle and cowboys replaced buffalo and Native Americans. Barbed wire fences went up all over the place to block off private property. Fields of crops grew in place of the prairie grass. Unfortunately these changes had

Buffalo Bill, a U.S. Army Scout who's real name was William Frederick Cody, is credited with giving the Wild West its name.

a negative impact on the Indians and the buffalo they relied on for food.

By the end of the nineteenth century, millions of people had made their way west. The government declared the frontier officially "closed" in the early 1890s. Even after this declaration was made, Americans in the East remained fascinated by the idea of the West and the frontier. Buffalo Bill's Wild West show played to sold-out crowds in eastern cities and dime novels about western adventures of Indian fighters and Pony Express riders were snatched up everywhere. Long after the frontier dust had settled behind the last wagon wheels, the mystique of the West, of exploring, expansion, and prosperity remained fresh in the mindset of all Americans.

WORD Round-Up

emigrant: A person who leaves one country or region to settle in another. Before Oregon and California were officially part of the United States, pioneers were called emigrants because they traveled outside U.S. territory once they crossed the Rocky Mountains.

prairie: The rolling land west of the Mississippi, with fertile soil covered by tall grass.

persecution: Harm or suffering inflicted on someone because they are different.

MAPPING THE WAY

ON JUNE 20, 1803, HAVING JUST MADE THE Louisiana Purchase, President Thomas Jefferson enlisted U.S. Army captains Meriwether Lewis and William Clark to lead an expedition called the Corps of Discovery. Their mission was to explore the Missouri River and to see if any of the waterways off the Missouri River led to the Pacific Ocean. Jefferson wanted to find the most direct water route to the West Coast, because he knew this would make it easier to transport goods from one side of the country to the other. He wanted the country to expand into the West. Jefferson also believed that a waterway to the Pacific would open up new opportunities for trade with countries in Asia.

The area of North America that had been settled, explored, and cleared for new communities lay between the East Coast and Ohio. To venture beyond this area was to go into territory where only a handful of European fur trappers

Captains Lewis and Clark holding a council with the Indians.

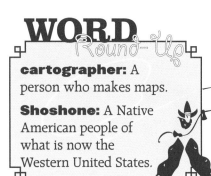

WORD Round-Up

cartographer: A person who makes maps.

Shoshone: A Native American people of what is now the Western United States.

had been before. There were scary rumors and stories about hostile Native Americans and massive animals that lived in this unexplored wilderness. Lewis and Clark were up to the task. They were adventurous by nature, and they were careful observers of the land around them. They were also skilled **cartographers**, which is one of the reasons Jefferson chose them for the expedition.

Throughout their remarkable journey, Lewis and Clark discovered and recorded in their journals 122 animals and 178 plants that were previously unknown to science. Along with their scientific observations, their accounts of the trail are filled with details of daily life and give us a look at what it was like to spend 28 months in uncharted territory. Throughout the expedition Lewis and Clark had to be very resourceful and

William Clark

The Journals of Lewis & Clark

Here are a few examples of life on the trail from their journals. Notice the different way they spoke and spelled.

JULY 30, 1805 "...having now secured my supper...I cooked my duck which I found very good and after eating it layed down and should have had a comfortable nights lodge but for the musquetoes which infested me all night..."

AUG. 2, 1805 "...we feasted sumptuously on our wild fruits, particularly the yellow currents and the deep purple service berries, which I found to be excellent...on our way we saw an abundance of deer [and] Antelopes, of the former we killed 2. We also saw many tracks of the Elk and bear, no recent appearance of Indians..."

JULY 16, 1806 "...saw a buffalow & Sent Shannon to kill it this buffalow provd to be very fat Bull I had most of the Flesh brought on and a part of the Skin to make mockersons for Some of our lame horses...and put on their feet which Seams to relieve them very much in passing over the Stony plains..."

Sacagawea

As a young girl Sacagawea was taken from her Shoshone family by a raiding Indian party of Minnetares. She eventually ended up the wife of Toussaint Charbonneau and accompanied him on the Lewis and Clark expedition. It is likely that Lewis and Clark were viewed as peaceful by Native American tribes because they had Sacagawea and her child with them. Sacagawea is only mentioned about 25 times in the extensive journals kept by the expedition, but the picture that emerges is one of a smart and helpful young woman. On top of her work as a translator, she taught Lewis and Clark about the nutritional and medicinal value of the native plants. Although Sacagawea clearly pulled her weight on this dangerous expedition—all the while caring for her infant son—she wasn't paid for her contributions.

Meriwether Lewis

prepared for the unknown, so they brought along a sewing kit, carpentry tools, and a portable forge.

Lewis and Clark hired Toussaint Charbonneau, a French trapper who was married to a young **Shoshone** woman named Sacagawea, to help them communicate with Native American tribes. First, Sacagawea would communicate with the Native Americans who spoke Shoshone. Then, she would translate the Native Americans' words to French for her husband. And from there, her husband would translate the French to English for Lewis and Clark. Sacagawea and Charbonneau's infant son, Jean

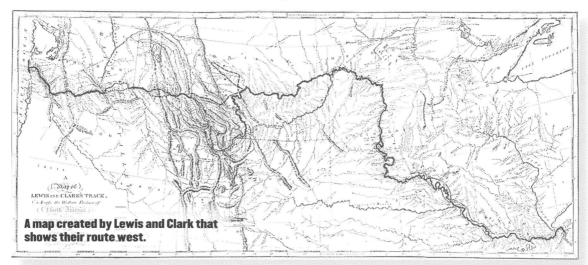

A map created by Lewis and Clark that shows their route west.

Baptiste was with them on the journey.

Throughout the journey William Clark worked on a map of the expedition that was engraved and published in 1814. This map was very accurate, which was most impressive considering that he created it without the technology available to cartographers

Mountain Men & Fur Traders

Lewis and Clark weren't the only white men traveling through the Northwest in the early part of the nineteenth century. Hundreds of trappers probed the lakes and rivers of the West in their quest for beaver pelts, which were very popular during this time period in clothing and hats. Many fur trappers called themselves "mountain men." Most of them dressed in buckskin clothes they had sewed themselves, and in general they had a wild and unkempt appearance. These mountain men hunted for the fur trading companies.

Two of the most famous fur trading companies were the Missouri Fur Company, based in St. Louis, and the American Fur Company, based in Astoria at the mouth of the Columbia River. A rival British company, the Hudson's Bay Company, was located at Fort Vancouver in what is now southwestern Washington. The fur companies would organize a rendezvous once a year during which the fur trappers would come to a central location to trade their skins for money and provisions. This rendezvous was also a time when fur trappers would trade gossip and wild stories.

By about 1840 the beaver had been over-trapped in many areas, so it was much harder to find them. At the same time, European fashion changed and beaver top hats were no longer fashionable. For these reasons many mountain men looked for a new line of work. Because they had an amazing knowledge of the West, many of them went on to become guides for the U.S. Army or for wagon trains.

today. Clark's map and information about the Corps of Discovery expedition provided many American pioneers with details about where they were headed and what they'd find along the way. Unfortunately, after 1805, the powerful Native American Blackfoot nation did not allow white travelers to pass through their territory in the Northern Plains, which included a portion of the trail that Lewis and Clark had mapped. So pioneers and mountain men were left to find a slightly different route. One of these routes became known as the Oregon Trail.

The stories and information that Lewis and Clark brought back from

John C. Fremont

John C. Fremont of the Army Topographical Corps led a surveying party of the region between the Missouri River and the Rocky Mountains in 1842. His surveying group was guided by mountain man Kit Carson. Thousands of Oregon Trail emigrants used Fremont's map and account of the expedition—which was published by Congress—as their guidebook to Oregon.

Guidebooks

Aside from the maps made by Lewis and Clark and John C. Fremont, how did easterners who didn't hire mountain men for guides, research the routes that led to the West? There were many guidebooks published in the nineteenth century that told of the riches that lay across the Mississippi River. For example, in 1845 Josiah T. Marshall published *Farmer's and Emigrant's Hand-book: Being a Full and Complete Guide for the Farmer and the Emigrant.* This book was almost 500 pages long and contained a vast variety of "Recipes, Hints, Tables, Facts, etc., to aid the Emigrant, whether male or female in daily life." Marshall's book was very helpful to pioneers, but not all of the guidebooks were as well done. Some were created by authors and publishers who had not even been out West themselves, but who wanted to make a quick dollar. Usually these guidebooks were misleading about which routes to take and what you could expect to find at the end of the trail.

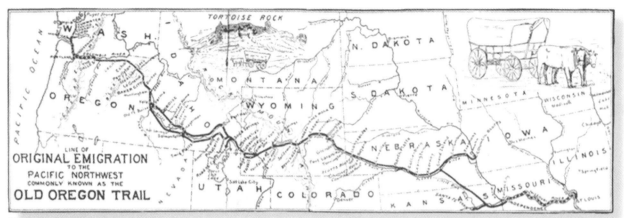

A map of the Oregon Trail.

their journey excited the imagination of many Americans. Tales of wide-open land and of rivers overflowing with fish got people thinking about moving from the increasingly crowded East to this beautiful land stocked with food and opportunity. And, over the course of the century, the lure of cheap land became an irresistible pull to thousands of Americans. The only question in the beginning was how to make this happen? Think about it, how do you cash in all your belongings and the life you have grown familiar with to trek across the country with your entire family to start over in a strange and wild place?

DID YOU KNOW?

The **Oregon Trail** was a famous route used by many American pioneers. It stretched 2,000 miles west from jumping off places along the Missouri River.

Make Your Own
SALT DOUGH MAP

Make this three-dimensional map and you'll have a better appreciation and understanding of where the Oregon Trail went.

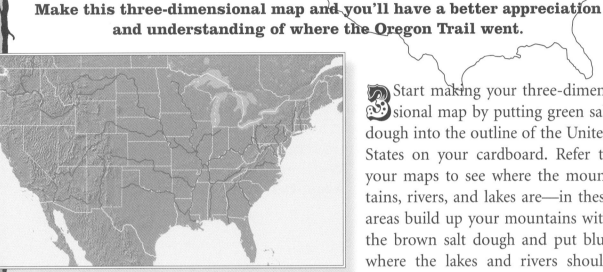

1 Blow the landforms map up to about 11 by 17 inches. Cut the outline of the United States out and trace around it on the cardboard with your pencil. Set aside.

2 Place the salt and flour in a bowl and add enough water to make a thick dough. Put the dough on a piece of waxed paper. Mix green food coloring into about two-thirds of the dough, and divide the remaining dough into two piles and mix in brown food coloring in one and blue in the other. Green is for most of the country, brown for mountains, and blue for water.

3 Start making your three-dimensional map by putting green salt dough into the outline of the United States on your cardboard. Refer to your maps to see where the mountains, rivers, and lakes are—in these areas build up your mountains with the brown salt dough and put blue where the lakes and rivers should be. Pay close attention to the geography of the western part of the United States and make sure you build the Rocky Mountains and put in the Great Salt Lake and some of the largest rivers like the Mississippi and the Missouri.

4 Let your map dry. Then mark the path of the Oregon Trail from Independence, Missouri, to Oregon with your black marker.

* go to www.eduplace.com and click on the outline maps, then United States, then United States physical OR go to www.worldatlas.com and keep clicking on North America and then United States to blow up the map.

SUPPLIES

* **maps of landforms of the United States***
* **piece of cardboard about 15 by 20 inches**
* **pencil**
* **2 cups of salt**
* **1 cup of flour**
* **water**
* **waxed paper**
* **food coloring (blue, green, brown)**
* **black permanent marker**
* **map of Oregon Trail**

Go on a
TREASURE HUNT

This activity will give you some idea of how difficult it is to follow someone else's directions. Many pioneers were following directions written in guidebooks giving information about where the trail went, where the good places were for water and grass, where rivers needed to be crossed, etc. But often something got lost or misunderstood in the translation. Let's see how good you are at giving and then following directions. This is a two-part activity that requires at least two people or two teams. One person or team is responsible for hiding the treasures and making up the directions. The other team follows the clues and retrieves the treasures. Then switch sides.

SUPPLIES

* 10 big colored plastic Easter eggs to hide things in
* small candy like Hershey kisses or jelly beans
* trinkets like plastic rings or necklaces
* small notebook
* pencil

1 Put the candy and trinkets inside the plastic eggs so you have 10 treasures to hide. Decide how far you're going to go on the treasure hunt—are you going to stay in the backyard or stay on one side of the street, or on the playground—so the seekers can't get too far off track.

2 The first team hides the eggs and makes up the clues, writing them down in the notebook. Be sure to include a lot of clues that rely on landmarks and directions. Clues can include things like how many steps it is from one egg to the next. Write something like, "Take 10 large steps toward Mrs. Jones's house then turn to your right and take four tiny steps. Turn and face the big bush by the front window and look to your left." Don't make it too simple.

3 Give the notebook to the seekers and let them try to find all the eggs. After one team finds all the eggs, have that team re-hide them and make up new clues.

Make Your Own

PEMMICAN

Pemmican was a traditional food eaten by Native Americans and adopted by the mountain men as they explored the frontier. The beauty of pemmican is that it was a high-energy, portable food. You could just stick some in your pouch and be on your way. The original pemmican recipe used bear grease, but we'll leave that out of our recipe.

1 Pound the beef jerky with the kitchen mallet on a cutting board until the jerky gets powdery. Add the dried fruit. With your pastry blender, chop and grind the dried fruit right into the jerky powder. You want to get the fruit and the meat as mixed as possible, so that you end up with a meat–fruit paste.

2 Place a piece of waxed paper on your cookie sheet and spread the mixture onto it. Place another piece of waxed paper on top. With your rolling pin, flatten your pemmican so it's about half an inch thick.

3 Leave the waxed paper on your pemmican, and move the cookie sheet to a sunny place. Let it dry for a day or two. At that point, break your pemmican into pieces and store in plastic baggies until you're ready to eat this high-energy Native American food.

SUPPLIES

2 ounces of beef jerky

kitchen mallet

cutting board

4 dried apple slices

1 handful of another dried fruit (maybe cranberries or raisins)

pastry blender

waxed paper

cookie sheet

rolling pin

plastic baggies

THE DECISION TO GO WEST

BETWEEN THE LOUISIANA PURCHASE AND OTHER territories given to the United States, the country suddenly grew much larger. By the middle of the 1800s most people in the United States believed in an idea of Manifest Destiny. What is Manifest Destiny? This idea said that it was the God-given right of Americans to settle and develop the West. How did it get its name? From a newspaperman named John Louis O'Sullivan in 1845. He wrote, "This American claim is by right of our manifest destiny to overspread and to possess the whole of the continent which Providence [meaning God] has given us."

While the idea of Manifest Destiny had been around for a long time,

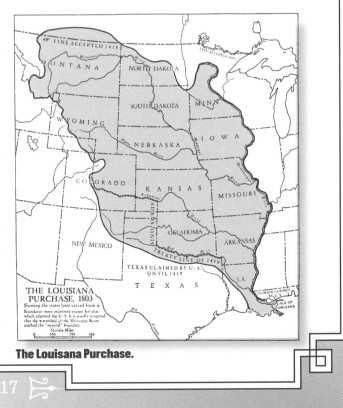

The Louisana Purchase.

General Taylor at the battle of Buena Vista during the Mexican-American War.

O'Sullivan made it more popular by giving it a name. At that time, President James K. Polk was pushing England and Mexico to give up their rights to land in the West. England gave up part of Oregon, but Mexico did not give up its lands in the Southwest and California without a fight. The people of Texas **seceded** from Mexico in 1836 to become an independent country called the Lone Star Republic. Then the area was **annexed** by the United States and became a state in 1845. Mexico went to war to try to get their former territory back. When Mexico lost, the punishment was that it had to give its territories to America for $15 million.

With Manifest Destiny on their minds, Americans could settle land in the deserts of the Southwest, the grassy prairies of the Great Plains, or the fertile valleys of the Northwest. It made them feel that it was okay to take the land. But what happened in the process of conquering the West? Americans drove Native American tribes from their homelands, putting an end to their cultures and way of life. Nothing stood in the way of Manifest Destiny.

As more and more western land became United States property, the government had to figure out a fair way to distribute it. So Congress passed something called the Preemption Act in 1830. It allowed settlers to buy up to 160 acres of public land. Pioneers had to build a shelter and improve the land by farming it for at least 12 months. Then they could buy the land for $1.25 per acre. This encouraged people to move west and improve the land for the benefit of the country. It also gave them protection from **land speculators**, who couldn't buy the land once settlers had been living on it. Land speculators grabbed as much land

secede: To quit, leave, or withdraw.

annex: To take possession or control of something.

land speculators: People who made money by claiming prairie land and then selling it to settlers.

homesteader: A person who settled and farmed land, especially under the Homestead Act.

Homesteaders

Homesteaders were pioneers who lived and farmed on public land. Under the Homestead Act of 1862, hopeful homesteaders paid a filing fee of $10 to homestead a particular plot of land. At the end of 5 years, a homesteader had to fill out a "proof" form. Two neighbors had to swear that the homesteader had indeed lived on the land and improved it. After the Civil War, former slaves were allowed to homestead. The only money that the homesteader had to pay was the filing fee.

as they could, hoping to resell it to the settlers for a profit.

When a pioneer decided to settle on an unclaimed spot of public land, he filed his claim with the nearest land office. This claim was proof that he and his family intended to live and work on the land. After a year, the settler went back to the land office and paid for his plot of improved land.

The Homestead Act of 1862 made it even easier to own land. A settler could get 640 acres and didn't have

Painting by John Gast, 1872. "America" is floating over the Plains bringing light to the dark and desolate landscape, showing the way for pioneers.

to pay for the land. The homesteader had to live on the land for 5 years. During that time he had to build a home and farm the land. After that, the land was theirs. Ten percent of the land in America was claimed and settled under provisions of the Homestead Act. The only rule was that the homesteader had to be a head of the household and at least 21 years old.

Advertising the West

Newspaper advertisements all over the country told about how wonderful the West was. *The Saint Louis Weekly* printed the following: "California has a perpetual spring . . . without the sultriness of summer or the chilling winds of winter . . . immense herd of wild cattle . . . a soil unsurpassed for richness and productiveness." Western towns often painted unrealistic pictures of their settlements in the newspapers, urging settlers to head west. This means they made it sound better

Laura Ingalls Wilder

In 1868 the Ingalls family moved to Kansas by covered wagon. Like many pioneer families, the Ingalls moved several more times and finally ended up in Dakota Territory. As an adult, Laura Ingalls Wilder was very good at recalling her childhood and the stories her father and mother told her back then. She often told them to her own daughter, Rose. When Laura Ingalls Wilder was in her sixties, Rose encouraged her to write these stories down. Her first book was published in 1932 when she was 65. She eventually wrote eight books in the *Little House on the Prairie* series. Millions of young readers over several generations have been introduced to the West and pioneer life by reading Laura Ingalls Wilder books. We can learn a lot about the pioneer experience from reading her books. They are full of details of everyday life, including life on the trail.

than it was. Along with newspaper advertisements, railroad companies promoted settlement along their railroad lines heading west. They printed pamphlets and broadside posters urging would-be homesteaders to travel west.

How else did people hear about the West? Through letters and word of mouth. It was very common for people to write back home to their friends and family, encouraging them to come out West too. Sometimes western settlements filled with people who had been neighbors in the East.

∞ Overheard: Laura Ingalls Wilder ∞

"They were going to Indian country. Pa said there were too many people in the Big Woods now . . . Wild animals would not stay in a country where there were so many people. Pa did not like to stay, either. He liked a country where the wild animals lived without being afraid . . . In the long winter evenings he talked to Ma about the Western country. In the West the land was level, and there were no trees. The grass grew thick and high. There the wild animals wandered and fed as though they were in a pasture that stretched much farther than a man could see, and there were no settlers. Only Indians lived there."

Little House in the Big Woods

⌒ Overheard ⌒

"One Saturday morning father said that he was going to hear Mr. Burnett talk about Oregon . . . Mr. Burnett hauled a box out on to the sidewalk, took his stand upon it, and began to tell us about the land flowing with milk and honey on the shores of the Pacific. Father was so moved by what he heard that he decided to join the company that was going west to Oregon."

Recollection from a farmer's son about why the family moved west

The Gold Rush

In 1848, people discovered gold in California. Prospectors from all over the country rushed to seek their fortune. This was called California Fever, or Gold Fever. The Gold Rush movement began when a man named John Sutter, who lived near modern-day Sacramento, rebuilt his gristmill. One of his workers looked down into the river and saw flashes of gold. He scooped up a couple of ounces of the precious metal, put it in a bottle, and showed it to his boss. News of the discovery spread quickly. Within weeks people arrived hoping to strike it rich.

Panning for gold.

Tens of thousands of **prospectors** and miners poured into California over the next couple of years. They were mostly single men between the ages of 20 and 40, called **Forty-Niners**, who took over the territory from the **Californios**.

⟩ Oklahoma Land Rush ⟨

In 1889, nearly two million acres of land in the heart of Indian Territory

were opened to homesteading by the federal government. One hundred thousand people lined up on the morning of April 22, ready to stake a claim when the bugles blew at noon. All the acres in the Oklahoma District were claimed by nightfall.

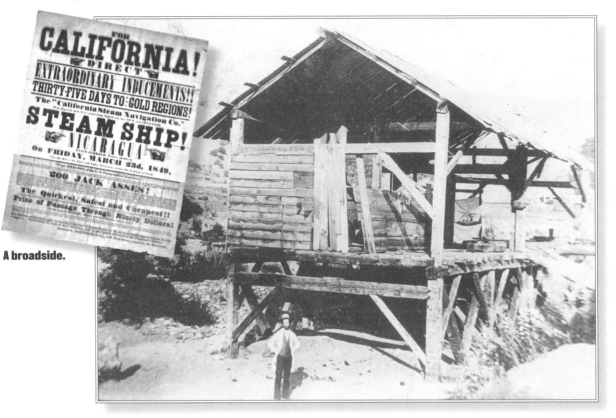

A broadside.

Sutter's Mill, a sawmill owned by nineteenth-century pioneer John Sutter, at the bank of the American River.

By the mid-1850s, there were nearly 300,000 gold seekers in the region. Most of these men never found gold, but they did change the area forever. The original gold strike at Sutter's Mill was about 100 miles northeast of San Francisco. In just over a year, San Francisco grew from 900 to 25,000 people. Think about what this kind of growth means to a town. All these people needed places to live and food to eat. Many towns in the area "boomed" overnight if gold was discovered nearby, but not all of them remained large and continued to grow like

Wild West ghost town Bodie, California. In 1876, the Standard Company discovered gold, which transformed Bodie from an isolated mining camp to a Wild West boomtown. By 1880 Bodie boasted a population of nearly 10,000.

John Sutter (1803–1880)

John Sutter came to the American West from Germany in search of fortune. For several years he worked as a trader on the Santa Fe Trail. Then he moved to California and established a settlement east of San Francisco along the Sacramento River. Sutter was granted nearly 50,000 acres for his settlement, and he built Sutter's Fort. This was a massive **adobe** structure with walls 18 feet high and 3 feet thick on the banks of a river he named the American River. Sutter's enormous ranch supported a herd of 13,000 cattle. Then, on January 24, 1848, one of his workmen, James Marshall, found gold nuggets in the American River. Sutter tried to get all of his employees to keep this discovery secret but soon word of gold leaked out. Gold seekers overran the ranch. Squatters occupied his land, butchered his cattle, and destroyed his crops. Sutter went bankrupt a few years later, and he spent the rest of his life trying to get the federal government to pay for the damage.

San Francisco. Some of them "busted" just as quickly as they'd boomed once the gold ran out.

The California Gold Rush attracted many people who did not plan to stay for long. Once they'd found their fortune they planned to return home rich. So the towns that sprung up around the mining areas were temporary, often built of shacks. Since no women or children lived there, these mining towns usually had no churches or schools. A miner or prospector's life consisted of working hard and playing hard, so these boomtowns had their share of saloons. The richest person in a boomtown wasn't always the prospector who found gold. The saloon keeper who sold food, whiskey, and other goods to the miners struck it rich too.

∞ Overheard: John Sutter ∞

"There is a saying that men will steal every-thing but a milestone and a millstone. They stole my millstones."

Word Round-Up

prospector: Someone who explores an area for valuable natural resources, like gold.

Forty-Niners: People who went to California in the rush for gold in 1849.

Californios: Spanish-speaking California natives who settled in the area many years before American emigrants arrived.

adobe: Building material of sun-dried earth and straw.

The Gold Rush town of Deadwood in the Dakota Territory, 1876.

Throughout the nineteenth century there were other gold strikes and silver strikes in western regions—in Nevada, Montana, and an area called the Black Hills in what is now South Dakota. These strikes, like the California strike, brought a rush of prospectors. The prospectors pushed out the Native Americans living there, and built up mining boomtowns where Native Americans used to live. When gold was discovered in the remote area of Cherry Creek in Colorado in 1858, the field of tents and crude cabins set up by prospectors developed into the city of Denver. By 1865, Denver had a population of 5,000 and was known as the Queen City of the Plains.

The Black Hills have always been sacred to the Lakota Sioux people. According to a treaty with the United States government, the Black Hills belonged to the Lakota. Yet when prospectors discovered gold there they ignored this treaty. Before long the Lakota had to make a choice: defend their territory with violent force or allow it to be overrun. The Lakota chose to fight for their land, and the most famous battle took place on June 25, 1876. This battle was named, "Custer's Last Stand" or "the Battle of the Little Bighorn." Lieutenant Colonel George Armstrong Custer and his cavalry were defeated in this battle. Despite their victory, and the brave leadership of Crazy Horse and Sitting Bull, the Native Americans were eventually forced to surrender.

Sitting Bull

Lieutenant Colonel G. A. Custer

Levi Jeans

In 1850 Levi Strauss moved to San Francisco. He sewed pants for gold miners out of a twilled cotton cloth known as "genes" in France. Metal rivets sewn on the pockets made them stronger. Although we now commonly refer to jeans as "blue jeans," they used to be dyed brown.

Patent drawing for Strauss's rivet method.

⌒ Overheard: Mark Twain ⌒

"I confess, without shame, that I expected to find masses of silver lying all about the ground. I expected to see it glittering in the sun on mountain summits. I was perfectly satisfied in my own mind as I could be of anything, that I was going to gather up, in a day or two, or at furthest a week or two, silver enough to make me satisfactorily wealthy—and so my fancy was already busy with plans for spending this money."

Mark Twain, who was lured to a new mining spot in Unionville, Nevada

Preparing for the Journey

Once a family decided to move Out West, they had to decide what to take and what to leave behind. There was limited space on the wagon trains and only so much weight that the horses or oxen could pull. Sadly, pioneers often had to leave behind more than just personal belongings. Older parents and grandparents often could not make the long journey. Pioneer families knew they might never see the people they left behind. This made parting with family possessions, including furniture made by family members, all the more difficult.

It cost about $500–$1,000 to equip a family for the journey, which in the mid-nineteenth century was an awful lot of money. That would equal about $12,500–$25,000 today. Those who didn't spend the money on food, a good wagon, and healthy oxen to pull it, risked starving on the trail or losing their wagons. To earn money for the trip, families sold everything, including their land and house, and they planned carefully for the trip.

Wagon train at rest. From Harper's Weekly, February 1864.

In general, pioneers planned to take at least 200 pounds of flour, 150 pounds of bacon packed in barrels, 20 pounds of sugar, 10 pounds of salt, and 10 pounds of coffee on their trip. They also carried dried fruits and vegetables. Even with all these provisions, though, pioneers still relied on hunting and trading with the Native Americans for fresh meat, fish, and vegetables.

Pioneers also packed as much as they could fit for the end of the journey. There was no guarantee the pioneers would be able to buy supplies where they settled. They would need seeds and a plow for planting, tools for clearing the land and building a new house, and spinning wheels and looms for making cloth. Other necessities included shoes, blankets, lanterns, needles, thread, mirrors, matches, writing paper and pens, and medicines. Families also brought their horses and livestock. The horses could be ridden, and the horses and cattle grazed along the way in the Great Plains. Oxen were the most common animal pioneers used to pull the covered wagons. They were slower than horses, but they had more power and stamina. At the end of the trail oxen could be used for heavy farm work like plowing.

A yolk of oxen.

Make Your Own BROADSIDE

Broadsides were posters that were often printed on thin paper or newsprint, and they announced everything from upcoming dances to free land available in the West. In this activity you'll make your own broadside advertising your favorite vacation spot. Your job is to make it appealing enough to make other people want to vacation there.

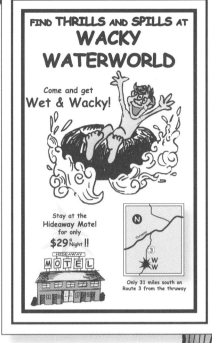

1 Read through all the brochures and information from the Internet that you've gathered about your vacation spot. Maybe take some notes on how much it costs to stay in the hotel, motel, or campsite, and what your favorite activities are (like sliding down a water slide, swimming in the ocean, or playing mini-golf).

2 Take your ruler and measure a half inch in from each side of your paper. Make a little mark every 6 inches and then use your pencil and ruler to make a faint border around your paper. Take your thick black marker and trace over your pencil border. Measure in another half-inch from your black border and make another faint pencil border. Using your thick black marker, trace over this inner pencil border.

3 Using your pencil and ruler make several faint horizontal lines on your paper—these are where you're going to write your information. Think

of an interesting "headline" to get people to read your broadside and write it with the thick black marker. If you're making a broadside about a water park, maybe write something like, "Find Thrills and Spills at Wacky Waterworld."

4 For the rest of the information you want to put on the broadside make sure you include how to get to your vacation spot (for example, "Only 31 miles south on Route 3 from the thruway"), and also include the best things you will find at the vacation spot.

5 Use your thin marker to write the rest of your information on your broadside. Use exclamation marks (for example, "Stay at the Hideaway Motel for only $29 a night!"), and if you feel particularly clever, make some little drawings on your broadside.

SUPPLIES

- information about your favorite vacation spot from maps, brochures, and the Internet
- ruler
- paper, preferably 11 by 17 inches
- pencil
- markers: thick black, thin black, and other colors

WAGON TRAINS

AFTER LEAVING THEIR HOMES, PIONEERS GATHERED AT **jumping-off places**. These were communities along the Missouri River where pioneer families formed a **wagon train**. Pioneer families didn't always make plans with other pioneer families ahead of time. Rather, they waited at a jumping-off point until enough wagons showed up to form a train. The pioneers wanted to have enough wagons in their wagon train to feel safe, but not so many wagons that they got bogged down as they traveled. There was no magic number of wagons in a wagon train. As wagon trains traveled along the trail, they often split into smaller groups of about four wagons each. Many wagon trains hired guides who had experience with the trail to help them find their way. Sometimes the guides were mountain men who used to trap for a living.

A wagon train heading west.

Pioneers needed to get on the trail by May. This way they could make the long journey to Oregon or California before it snowed in the Western mountains in the fall. Another reason is that pioneers who left later in the season would find the grass along the trail eaten by the live-stock of pioneers who had left before them. If the animals had to graze farther from the trail it made the journey slower. This put the pioneers at an even greater risk of getting caught in the mountain snows later in the year.

Word
Round-Up

jumping-off places: Towns along the Missouri River, including Independence, St. Joseph, and Kansas City, that served as gathering spots for pioneer families who wanted to join a wagon train.

wagon train: A group of wagons that traveled across the country in a line.

buffalo chips: The name given to dried buffalo dung that was gathered by children and used for fuel while on the trail. It burned hot and clean.

Moving Along the Trail

Everyone had jobs and responsibilities on the trail. Before a wagon train left a jumping-off place all the men got together and decided on the rules to follow. They also decided what jobs everyone would do while out on the trail. They elected a captain to enforce the rules. Many pioneers were single young men (and there were even a few single young women) who would join up with another family. They would work for the family in exchange for food.

A few men in each wagon train were picked to be scouts and hunters. Scouts rode far ahead of a wagon train looking for landmarks to help keep the pioneers on

Covered Wagons

Covered wagons were about 10 feet long and 4 feet wide. They were covered by canvas laid over the top of a wooden hoop frame. A team of oxen usually pulled the wagon, which held most of a family's food and supplies for the 4- or 5-month journey. They could hold up to 2,500 pounds of supplies. Some families traveled with more than one wagon. Covered wagons were often called prairie schooners because the white canvas tops looked like sails moving through a sea of prairie grass.

DID YOU KNOW?

An ox yoke is a wooden bar that links two oxen together. This team of oxen would then be attached to the wagon. There were no reins so oxen were often guided by a pioneer walking beside them.

track. They also kept their eyes open for trouble, such as a dangerous river or a band of hostile Native Americans. The hunters searched for deer, antelope, or buffalo to kill for the evening meals. The rest of the men traveled with the wagon train. They guided the oxen, herded the loose horses and livestock, and took turns standing guard at night.

Everybody walked the entire length of the trail unless they were too old, too sick, or too young to walk. Try to imagine walking about 15 to 20 miles every day for 5 months. You would walk for more than 2,000 miles. The pioneers covered the most ground when they walked through the prairie, a huge, grassy area without trees. It stretched for hundreds of miles in every direction. Some pioneers said it was like walking through an ocean of grass. The pioneers traveled slowest through the mountains.

In many ways, women had the toughest time out on the trail. They had to cook every meal over an open fire. Some of them had never done this before! They also packed and unpacked the wagons every day, mended the clothes, and washed the clothes whenever possible. On top of all this, many women had to care for babies or young children. It was common for a woman to give birth while on the trail. The wagon train could only afford to stop for one day while a woman gave birth, and then they were on their bumpy way again.

Children also had responsibilities. Older girls helped their mothers with the cooking and sewing and caring for younger children. Older boys helped their fathers herd livestock. Some-

Prairie Dogs

Children were fascinated by the prairie dogs that lived on the High Plains. These small burrowing rodents are natives of the grasslands west of the Mississippi River. They're 12 to 16 inches long and are highly social animals that live in "towns," which are clusters of holes connected by underground tunnels. Prairie dog sentries sit on the edge of the prairie dog village and whistle when they spot danger.

A pioneer mother and daughter collect buffalo chips for fuel.

times older boys were allowed to go with the hunters. This was seen as a great honor. Younger children gathered **buffalo chips** for fuel and kept the milk bucket full of cream. Hanging on the back of the moving wagon all day, a bucket of cream would slosh around and churn itself into butter.

A Typical Day on the Trail

Day-to-day life on the trail was difficult. It could also be really boring. To the traveling pioneer, the prairie seemed to stretch on forever, like a vast sea of tall grass. The wagon train would move forward about 25 miles on a very good day of travel, but the average daily distance the pioneers traveled was closer to 15 miles. Sometimes families would get into arguments, and the wagon trains would split up. This didn't happen often, but when it did, it was important to try and stay with an experienced guide.

Pioneers slept under wagons or in tents. A typical day began at 4 a.m. when the guards fired rifles into the air to wake everyone up. While the men and older boys rounded up the cattle that grazed inside the **corral** at night, the women prepared a breakfast of bread, bacon, and beans. Sometimes they made johnnycakes or corn porridge. After the meal the women cleaned up breakfast and packed up the wagon. The men would take down the tents.

By 7 a.m. each family would have their oxen yoked and attached to the wagon. Then they moved their wagons in place. Their place in line rotated each day, moving up a spot so that no one got stuck permanently at the back of the line where it was so dusty it was hard to see or breathe. A trumpet signaled the wagon train to move forward. All of the livestock followed the last wagon.

Word
Round-Up

corral: An enclosure formed by a circle of wagons, mainly to keep the livestock safe from coyotes.

skillet: A cast-iron frying pan.

Dutch oven: A heavy cast-iron pot with a tight-fitting lid that was used for baking as well as cooking. Heaping coals on top created a more even heat, baking whatever was inside.

Midday was also called "Nooning time." The pioneers and animals got to eat and take a break. When the wagons began to roll again the kids would search for buffalo chips for fuel. They had to make sure not to go too far from the wagon train because there was always danger of getting lost in the sea of prairie grass. Being left behind was every child's worst nightmare.

By about 5 p.m. the scouts would choose the best spot to set up camp. All of the wagons would pull into a tight circle at this location, forming a corral. People pitched tents behind the wagons, and built fires with the buffalo chips that had been gathered by the children. The women made the evening dinner. Finally, by about 8 p.m., dinner was cleared away and guard duty began. The camp settled down for the evening.

Native Americans along the Trail

When pioneers began their journey west, many of them were afraid of being killed by Native Americans because of scary stories and rumors they had heard. In reality, most of the pioneers found the Native Americans to be helpful along the trail. Pioneers traded with them for fresh meat and vegetables, and Native Americans often helped guide the wagon trains. Native Americans also helped the pioneers cross rivers and pull wagons up steep hills as they traveled through difficult terrain.

Food on the Trail

Pioneers ate bread, beans, and bacon for all three meals, unless there was fresh meat. Women had to learn how to make bread on the trail using a **skillet** or a **Dutch oven**. Everyone drank coffee, even the children. Before the westward movement the water along the trail may have been fresh and clear. But thousands of pioneers and their livestock passed by, tromping through the rivers and using them for washing up. The water filled with bacteria that could make the travelers sick or even die. Boiling the water to make coffee made the water safer to drink by killing much of the bad bacteria. Besides, the coffee color and taste probably hid the brown color and bad taste of the water.

Native American Pictographs

Throughout the West you can find pictographs and petroglyphs on rocks. Pictographs are paintings on rock surfaces and petroglyphs are carvings in rock surfaces—you can imagine which one took longer to make. Native Americans made this "rock art." Most pictographs are under overhangs or in caves where they have been protected from the weather.

Sometimes the pictographs show animals, other times human figures or geometric designs. These images seemed very mysterious to pioneers. While it will never be known for certain, archaeologists think the Native Americans were recording successful hunts or significant events in their own lives or the life of their tribe. Many of these markings are thousands of years old.

Pioneers also left carvings and paintings as they traveled through the West. It was common for pioneers to carve their names and the date as they passed certain landmarks. Independence Rock, in Wyoming, was an important landmark on the route to Oregon and California. Pioneers tried to make it there by July 4 (see how the rock got its name?) so that they could reach their destination before the fall snows.

Make Your Own

COVERED WAGON

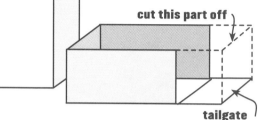

cut this part off

tailgate

1 Open the milk carton all the way so that you have a rectangle with one square opening on the top. Wash it out thoroughly. Cut one long side off the milk carton. Make a "tailgate" for the back of the wagon by cutting off the two short parts that were once folded at the top of the carton, leaving a flap that can be folded up for the tailgate.

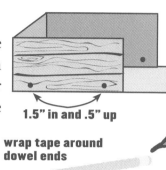

1.5" in and .5" up

wrap tape around dowel ends

the bottom of the wagon body. Punch holes at these four marks using the point of your scissors. These are where the wheels will attach. Measure the width of the bottom of your wagon and cut your dowels about a quarter-inch longer. Wrap an inch-long piece of tape around each end of the dowels. Put a push pin through the center of one plastic lid and push it into the end of the dowel. Place your dowel through the holes in the wagon and attach a wheel on the other end in the same way.

2 Cover the carton with brown paper using tape or glue. You can draw horizontal lines on the paper to make it look like the wagon is made out of wooden boards.

3 On each long side, measure 1½ inches in from each end and up a half-inch from

SUPPLIES

* ½-gallon cardboard milk carton
* scissors
* brown construction paper OR a brown paper bag
* tape OR Elmer's glue
* black thin line marker
* ruler
* 2 dowels
* 4 push pins
* 4 plastic lids from yogurt containers for wheels
* six 12-inch pipe cleaners
* white construction paper OR white cloth
* leather lace

4 To make the hoops for the cover of your wagon, bend the

pipe cleaners

pipe cleaners into half circles. Tape the ends to the inside of the wagon body. Try to make them evenly spaced and at an even height.

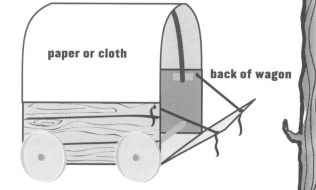

5 Cut the white construction paper or cloth to measure 7½ by 10 inches. Tuck the sides of your white rectangle down between the pipe cleaner hoops and the sides of the wagon bed. Tape a couple of places to hold it in place.

6 Poke a hole in both corners of the tailgate, then poke a hole on either side of the wagon bed in the back. Cut two pieces of leather lace about 4 inches long each and tie a knot at one end of each piece. Thread the lace through the front of the flap on each side so that the knot rests on the front of the tailgate then thread the lace through the side hole. This way you can raise or lower your tailgate.

Make Your Own PICTOGRAPH

1 Paint your river rocks with the light-colored acrylic paint using the large brush. Let dry. With your pencil, draw a design like a Native American pictograph. Or write your name and the date like an American pioneer would have done on Independence Rock.

2 Using the small paintbrush go over your pencil design with the dark-colored paint.

SUPPLIES

flat stones like river rocks, about 6 inches across

light acrylic paint

large paintbrush

pencil

small paintbrush

dark acrylic paint

Make Your Own
BUTTER

What cows eat affects the color and taste of butter made from their cream. The pioneers needed to be careful to keep the cows away from the wild onions and garlic! While on the trail, pioneers discovered that if they milked the cow in the morning and put the cream in a bucket hung from the back of the wagon, by the end of the day all the jostling would have turned the cream into butter.

1 Leave the whipping cream out so it comes to room temperature, and then pour it into the jar. Shake vigorously for about 10 minutes. The cream will separate into lumps of butter and some bluish-white liquid, which is buttermilk. The longer you shake, the more butter clumps you get.

2 Pour the butter and buttermilk into your glass bowl. Very carefully pour off the buttermilk. Rinse the butter clumps with cold water. Press the butter against the side of the bowl with a wooden spoon (do not use a metal spoon because your butter will pick up a metallic taste) and rinse with cold water until the water runs clear. This gets rid of any remaining buttermilk.

3 Taste the butter and add a dash of salt. Do you notice anything different about your butter? Look at the color. You can mix in a drop of yellow food coloring if you like.

SUPPLIES

- 1 pint of whipping cream
- glass jar with a secure lid
- glass bowl
- wooden (not metal) spoon
- salt
- yellow food coloring (optional)

HARDSHIPS ON THE TRAIL

LIFE OUT ON THE TRAIL WAS MORE THAN JUST DIFFICULT. It could also be very dangerous. One out of every 10 pioneers died on the journey west.

Diseases like cholera, malaria, smallpox, and diphtheria killed many people. When the pioneers got sick, most of them had fevers, diarrhea, and **delirium**. The different illnesses were all grouped together, commonly called "trail fever." Because this was before we knew what caused many illnesses, the pioneers didn't know how to avoid catching them.

When pioneers got sick on the trail, they were cared for by members of their family. There was no doctor to go to for help. Pioneer women knew some folk medicine and would make **poultices** and teas of herbs to treat everything from pneumonia to wounds. Snakebites were common and people treated snakebites in lots of different ways. One way was to cut a chicken in two and put it on the spot where the snake bit to draw out to the poison. Another involved drinking as much whiskey as possible.

Cholera is a disease caused by drinking polluted water or eating food infected by someone with cholera. This disease spread quickly through many wagon trains. Cholera causes severe diarrhea, vomiting, and leg cramps, and a person can die within hours of the first symptoms. Often, many members of the same family would die.

Many pioneers became sick with what they called "ague," which we now know was malaria. People catch malaria from mosquitoes. People with malaria might feel fine one day but have a chill the next day that causes them to shake so badly that their teeth clatter. Along with the shakes, the sick person runs a fever and has terrible muscle and head pain. The effects of malaria can last for years, so even if people with malaria get better, they might have spells of symptoms later.

Mormon settlers wrote about catching mountain fever outside of Salt Lake City. Settlers would complain of fever, muscle aches, joint pain, and sensitivity to the light. These symptoms could come back periodically for years. Some think it might have been typhoid fever but others think it could have been a disease caused by an insect, such as a tick. Today, there is a disease known as Rocky Mountain Spotted Fever that we know for sure is caused by a tick, and the symptoms are similar.

Rocky Mountain spotted fever tick.

Nature's Challenges

In 1844, a group known as the Stevens party was the first to get their wagons across the Sierra Nevada and all the way to what is now Sacramento, California. When they reached what would later be called the Donner Pass in the Sierra Nevada it was mid-November and the snow was 2 feet deep. In order to get their wagons up the steep mountains, these pioneers unloaded all of their wagons and carried everything to the summit. At the summit, the oxen were unhitched from the empty wagons and squeezed one at a time up a wide crack in a 10-foot high

granite wall. The travelers then chained the oxen to the wagons still below. As the oxen pulled the wagons, the men pushed, and eventually the wagons were inched over the wall.

Pioneers had to be resourceful when it came to crossing rivers. Remember, there were no bridges and if a shallow spot couldn't be found, pioneers had to figure out how to get themselves, their animals, and their wagons across without being swept downstream or drowning. One way pioneers kept the contents of their wagons dry was to take a couple of "fresh" buffalo hides and sew them together so they were big enough to cover the bed of a wagon. Then they dried the hides by stretching them across the wagon bed. Once these hides were thoroughly dry, the pioneers would rub **tallow** and ashes into the hides to make them more waterproof. If a river crossing was particularly dangerous, pioneers would sometimes chain their wagons together to make sure none of them were washed away.

Buffalo hide.

At the end of the Oregon Trail, the pioneers had to make rafts to ferry their wagons down the Columbia River. They cut down trees and lashed them together into rafts that were big enough to hold wagons.

Death on the Trail

Sadly, life on the trail was dangerous. People died from illnesses, hunting accidents, drowning, stampeding cattle, falling under wagon wheels, drinking bad water, thirst, starvation, and more. Life on the trail was very hard to begin with, so it was especially hard when a family member died.

When someone died on the wagon train, there was very little time to stop and mourn. Wood was so scarce that bodies were simply wrapped in canvas and buried along the trail. Some families wanted their loved ones buried right on the trail so that the wagon tracks and ruts would erase signs of a burial. They did that so wolves would not dig up the bodies. Pioneer graves marked by stones still stand along portions of the Oregon Trail today.

Stone marker along the Oregon Trail.

Word
Round-Up

delirium: Confusion and disorientation.

poultice: A medicinal concoction spread on a cloth that is applied to the skin to treat inflamed areas or improve circulation.

tallow: Melted animal fat used for making candles and soap, as well as waterproofing things.

They would then use poles to guide the rafts down the river. At this point in the journey the pioneers had been traveling for months and were exhausted. It took all of their energy just to stay alive during their terrifying river journey.

Pioneers had to watch the weather closely while they were on the trail. Calm rivers could become raging torrents after a hard thunderstorm and the dry, dusty trail could turn into knee-deep mud. Violent thunderstorms with heavy rains, hail, and scary lightning were common on the Plains in summer. If a wagon train left too late in the season, it could get trapped by fall blizzards and deep snow in the Western mountains.

∞ Overheard: Francis Parkman ∞

"Sometimes we passed the grave of one who had sickened and died on the way. The earth was usually torn up, and covered thickly with wolf-tracks. Some had escaped this violation. One morning, a piece of plank, standing upright on the summit of a grassy hill, attracted our notice, and riding up to it, we found the following words very roughly traced upon it, apparently with a red-hot iron: Mary Ellis, Died May 7, 1845. Aged two months."

From a series of articles Parkman wrote for
Knickerbocker *magazine, 1846–48*

Poor Guides and Guidebooks

Guides led wagon trains across the country. They were paid money by each family or single person who wanted to travel west. Many of the earliest guides were former mountain men, but later, many of the guides were men who had made the trip several times. Some guides didn't know much about the trail. Some even abandoned the wagon trains they had promised to guide safely. Then the pioneers had to struggle ahead on their own and hope that another wagon train would let them tag along, if they were lucky enough to find one. Other times

a guide might take a wagon train over a "shortcut" that he had read about but hadn't actually traveled. The wagon train could waste valuable time searching for the shortcut. As the trails became more established, guides became less crucial because pioneers could follow the well-worn ruts of earlier wagons.

∞ Overheard: Francis Parkman ∞

"Many were murmuring against the leader they had chosen, and wished to depose him; and this discontent was fomented by some ambitious spirits, who had hopes of succeeding in his place. The women were divided between regrets for the homes they had left and fear of the deserts and savages before them."

From a series of articles Parkman wrote for

Knickerbocker *magazine, 1846–48*

Both pioneers and new guides had to be careful of the many guidebooks being published. Some of the trail guidebooks were written by people who had never been on the trail. They simply gathered information from other reports

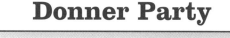

Donner Party

One wagon train that became famous for having a terrible guide was the Donner Party. After their guide led them on what he thought was a "shortcut," a trail he had only read about, the wagon train got trapped by blizzards and deep snow in the Sierra Nevada in early November. Some of the pioneers built cabins for shelter while others tried to live in tents. Fifteen of the men left the camp in mid-December on snowshoes to find help. Seven of them made it to Johnson's Ranch in the Bear River Valley a month later. A rescue party carrying supplies left the ranch on February 4 and arrived

The Donner Party struggles through the Sierra Nevada.

at Donner Lake two weeks later. Rescuers had to carry all the supplies on their backs because the snow in Donner Pass was 30 feet deep and horses couldn't get through. When the rescuers reached the trapped wagon train only 45 of the original 89 settlers were alive.

and printed their own book. Some guidebooks had inaccurate maps, which could have disastrous results for wagon trains trying to follow them. One of the most helpful guidebooks was a 24-page booklet written in 1848 by William Clayton. It had the impossibly long title that says it all—*The Latter-Day Saints' Emigrants' Guide: Being a Table of Distances, Showing All the Springs, Creeks, Rivers, Hills, Mountains, Camping Places, and All Other Notable Places, from Council Bluffs, to the Valley of the Great Salt Lake.*

Over-packing

During the beginning of the California Gold Rush a fortune hunter wrote home that he counted over a thousand abandoned wagons on his trip west along the California Trail. Along one 3-mile stretch, another pioneer counted 500 dead oxen (try to imagine what that smelled like!). He wrote in his journal that he saw trunks, clothing, shoes, and even food left behind as those caught up in gold fever pushed their party to go faster and faster. But the main reason why wagons, oxen, furniture and belongings of every kind got left on the trail was that people packed too many of their belongings before they left home.

Over-packing could cause a chain of unfortunate events. First, it meant that their oxen had to pull too much weight, which wore them out. That could make it easier for the oxen to get sick and die—especially if they didn't get extra food, which they often didn't. If their oxen died, people had to leave their wagons and carry everything they could while they walked. This made them more tired, hungry, and sick, as well. As these pioneers moved forward on foot, they had to toss aside much of what they were carrying so that they didn't use up all of their energy.

During the gold rush years, people raced each other to the gold Out West. In the rush, pioneers left things behind. They would often burn what they left so that no one else would benefit from it and potentially beat them to the gold fields.

DID YOU KNOW?

After years of people throwing things out of their wagons, wagon trains no longer had to hire guides—not only because the wagons could follow the deep ruts of the trails, but because the way was marked by piles of trash.

Make Your Own

JOURNAL

A lot of what we know about life on the trail comes from journals, diaries, and letters written by pioneers. Although the earliest explorers wrote on things like buckskin and calfskin, pioneers usually had access to some kind of paper. Their accounts of daily life are windows to the past and remind us how important it is to record even the most simple things about our day. Your job is to record your daily life for at least one week, so that 150 years from now, someone can look at your journal and see what it was like to live at the beginning of the twenty-first century.

1 Fold the pieces of white paper in half, widthwise. Now you will have paper that is 8½ by 7 inches.

2 Cut the brown paper bag into two 8½-by-10-inch pieces. Crumple, crush, and roll the paper bag sheets so they soften up. As you roll and crumple the paper, the fibers will get as soft as cloth material.

Be gentler with the paper as it becomes softer. Spread the pieces out flat.

3 Cut the pieces of cardboard into 7-by-9-inch rectangles. Put glue on one side of each of the cardboard pieces. It doesn't matter which side because you will cover it up.

4 Turn over each cardboard piece so the gluey side is down. Center each on one of the pieces of brown paper. Push down

SUPPLIES

* 10 pieces of 8½-by-14-inch white paper
* large brown grocery bag
* scissors
* ruler
* 2 pieces of cardboard (a cracker box or cereal box works great)
* glue stick, paste, or white glue
* 2 pieces of colored paper (old wrapping paper is great), cut to 6½ by 8 inches
* hole punch
* 3 brads or 3 rubber bands

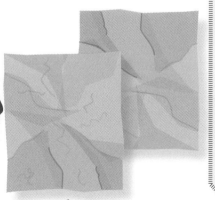

cardboard glued to brown paper

on the cardboard to make sure it sticks tight to the brown paper.

glue on extra brown paper

fold over extra brown paper

5 Cut the corners out from each brown paper corner to each cardboard corner. This will make it easy to fold over the extra brown paper onto the cardboard. Put glue on the extra brown paper surrounding the cardboard and fold it over onto the cardboard.

6 Put glue on one side of the colored paper and with the gluey side down, center the colored paper over the cardboard. This will cover up the rest of the cardboard and make a nice inside lining to your cover. Your cover is ready to be decorated!

glue colored paper over cardboard

7 Use the hole punch to punch three holes about one inch from the fold on the white paper. These will be your journal pages. Make sure the holes are in the same place on all 10 sheets of paper. The holes go on the left of your journal.

8 Put the folded white paper inside the front and back covers of your journal. Mark on the inside of the covers where the holes in the paper are. Punch matching holes in the cover so when you put the paper inside the covers you can see straight through all of them.

9 If you are using brads to complete your journal, you can fit them in each hole and fasten them onto the back cover. If you are using rubber bands, put one end of the rubber band through each hole and pull it through the other end of the rubber band. That will hold it tight. You can also use yarn, string, or even a cut-up shoelace!

POPULAR ROUTES

N 1832 NATHANIAL J. WYETH TOOK A PARTY OF AMERICAN traders to the Oregon territory. He hired mountain man William Sublette as his guide. Sublette knew he couldn't use Lewis and Clark's route because it went through the Blackfoot nation territory. Their territory was now off-limits to white travelers.

The Oregon Trail

Wyeth chose a different route, one that led through the western mountains on trails that animals and Native Americans had used for centuries. This trail became known as the Oregon Trail. Thousands of travelers moved west via the Oregon Trail.

Wyeth was amazed by all the fish—especially salmon—in the Columbia and Willamette Rivers in Oregon. He decided to head Back East to get equipment so he could start a business catching and drying fish in Oregon. When he returned West he stopped in what is now part of Idaho. With help from his men, Wyeth built Fort Hall, where they left their wagons. Wyeth used pack animals for the

Inside Fort Hall.

rest of his journey. In the coming decades, Fort Hall would be an important landmark and supply station for the pioneers traveling along the Oregon Trail.

In 1836 Dr. Marcus Whitman and Reverend Henry Spalding went to the Oregon territories with their wives, Narcissa and Eliza, to build a mission near the Columbia River. They planned to convert the Native Americans to Christianity. The women of the Whitman party were the first white women to cross the Rocky Mountains, and the party as a whole was the first to make the entire journey by wagon. Their trip proved that it was possible to transport a group's possessions all the way to the West by wagon.

In 1843, mountain men Jim Bridger and Louis Vasquez established Fort Bridger near the **Continental Divide** in present-day Wyoming. Fort Bridger became another important supply station for pioneers traveling the Oregon Trail. That same year, the **Great Migration**—a wagon train of more than 100 wagons and 5,000 head of cattle—left Independence, Missouri, under the guidance of Marcus Whitman. Whitman led them along the Oregon Trail, past Fort Bridger, and then on to the Willamette Valley in Oregon. From 1843 on, thousands of pioneers made the 2,000-mile-long trek along the Oregon Trail.

Narcissa & Dr. Marcus Whitman

∽ Overheard ∽

"I have no doubt our greatest work is to aid the white settlement of this country and help to found its religious institutions."

Marcus Whitman in a letter sent east from the missionary in Oregon

As pioneers headed west on the Oregon Trail, they passed several landmarks. The first came about 650 miles out of Independence, Missouri. It was known as

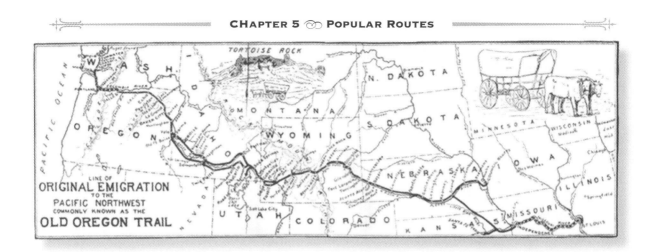

Chimney Rock, and it was a large pyramid-shaped reddish rock with a 100-foot spire that could be seen from 50 miles away. Chimney Rock was a welcome change of scenery—not only because the pioneers had traveled through hundreds of miles of nothing but prairie grass, but also because it meant they were moving closer toward their goal. Eventually the trail met up with the Platte River (called "Big Muddy" by the pioneers). The pioneers followed the "Big Muddy" for the next 450 miles through modern-day Nebraska into Wyoming. There they took a much-needed rest at **Fort Laramie**. As the pioneers approached the mountains, the tall prairie grass of the Great Plains gave way to shorter grass, and lots of buffalo, antelope, and prairie dogs. This region is sometimes referred to as the High Plains.

Further down the trail, in present-day southwestern Wyoming, was Independence Rock. This is a huge, dome-shaped rock. Thousands of trappers, mountain men, and pioneers scratched their names onto Independence Rock as they passed by. Because so many people "signed" the rock, some people called this the "Great Register of the Oregon Trail."

Word Round-Up

The Continental Divide: The high ground in the Rocky Mountains. On the east side the rivers flow toward the Mississippi River. On the west side the rivers flow toward the Pacific Ocean.

The Great Migration: The first large wagon train to travel the length of the Oregon Trail. It contained more than 100 wagons and 5,000 head of cattle.

Fort Laramie: A trading fort overlooking the Platte River in present-day Wyoming. It served as a valuable stopping point for pioneers who were exhausted and running out of food.

drought: A long period without rain that can often cause extensive damage to crops.

Chimney Rock.

The Great Plains

The Great Plains is the name for the enormous prairie in the middle of the United States and Canada. This area lies roughly between the Mississippi River and the Rocky Mountains. In the United States the Great Plains make up much of present-day New Mexico, Texas, Oklahoma, Colorado, Kansas,

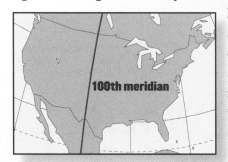

100th meridian

Nebraska, Wyoming, Montana, South Dakota, and North Dakota. Grasses almost 6 feet tall covered the region before the land was settled and farmed. The Great Plains generally lie from a bit east of the 100th meridian, which is the longitude line running down through the center of the country, to the Rocky Mountains. The Plains are vast and dry, so it was named the Great American Desert by some early explorers. The lack of rainfall means the Plains often have **droughts** and terrible dust storms, like the Dust Bowl during the 1930s. The Plains Indians included the tribes of the Blackfoot, Crow, Lakota, Cheyenne, Arapaho, and Comanche. This area was also home to most of the country's buffalo, until over-hunting destroyed the buffalo population. They were almost extinct by the 1880s.

The Mormon Trail

Between 1846 and 1868 almost 50,000 Mormon pioneers traveled to the Great Salt Lake region in what is now Utah. A man named Joseph Smith had founded the Mormon religion, also called the Church of Latter Day Saints, in upstate New York in the 1830s. The Mormons did not feel welcome there, so they pushed west in search of a place where they could practice their religion freely. They first settled in Illinois and built the town of Nauvoo. There were problems here too. When their founder was murdered there in 1844, the Mormons decided to pack up and head to the other side of the Rocky Mountains where they could start their religious community.

In 1846, Brigham Young led 15,000 Mormons to a place near present-day Omaha, Nebraska, where they set up a temporary village called Winter Quarters. This became

Joseph Smith

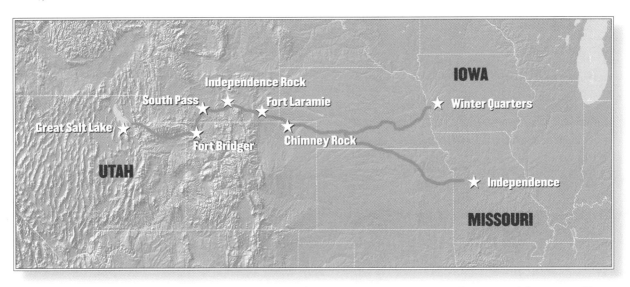

a Mormon jumping-off place. From there, Young continued west with a small party in search of what he called Zion. When they saw the Great Salt Lake in Utah territory they believed it to be their promised land, because it was beautiful and far away from outsiders.

The Mormon pioneers created a trail to the Great Salt Lake basin that came to be known as the Mormon Trail. Much of the Mormon Trail paralleled the Oregon Trail as far as Fort Bridger in modern-day Wyoming. At that point the Mormon Trail headed south and up over the Wasatch Mountains before heading down into the Great Salt Lake basin. The church sent missionaries to Europe to invite Mormons to come to the new Promised Land. They offered to give supplies to anyone willing to become a Mormon if they committed to making the long, hard journey.

Handcart train along the Mormon Trail.

Outfitting several thousand people per year with wagons and livestock was expensive. In 1856 the Mormon Church decided to outfit people willing to join them in Salt Lake with smaller, less expensive, two-wheeled handcarts—much like the pushcarts used by street vendors in New York City, only lighter. Amazingly, about 3,000 people walked the entire way pushing handcarts in front of them that held all their belongings. Wagons also went on the handcart train, but there was only one wagon for every 20 handcarts. One song from the Mormon handcart migration said, "Some may push and some may pull," and this was the case as they crossed thousands of miles in search of the Promised Land. It was a very difficult way to travel, and families were in big trouble if the father or oldest sons—the ones who usually pushed or pulled the cart—got injured or sick, or died.

Overheard: Jon Chislett

"Our seventeen pounds of clothing and bedding was now altogether insufficient for our comfort. Nearly all suffered more or less at night from cold. Instead of getting up in the morning strong, refreshed, vigorous, and prepared for the hardships of another day of toil, the poor Saints were to be seen crawling out from their tents haggard, benumbed, and showing an utter lack of that vitality so necessary to our success."

From Chislett's journal kept while leading a group of Mormon emigrants in the Great Handcart Migration of 1856.

Water Routes

Pioneers traveling to California in the first half of the nineteenth century did not always travel over land. They could board a ship in a city along the Atlantic coast and sail all the way around Cape Horn on the southern tip of South America. From Cape Horn they would turn north again and sail up the west coast of South America and Mexico until they reached California. This trip was expensive, dangerously stormy, and uncomfortable.

Another water route involved sailing down to Panama, crossing the narrow part of Panama by land, and then picking up a ship on the other side to complete the journey by sea along the Mexican Coast up to California.

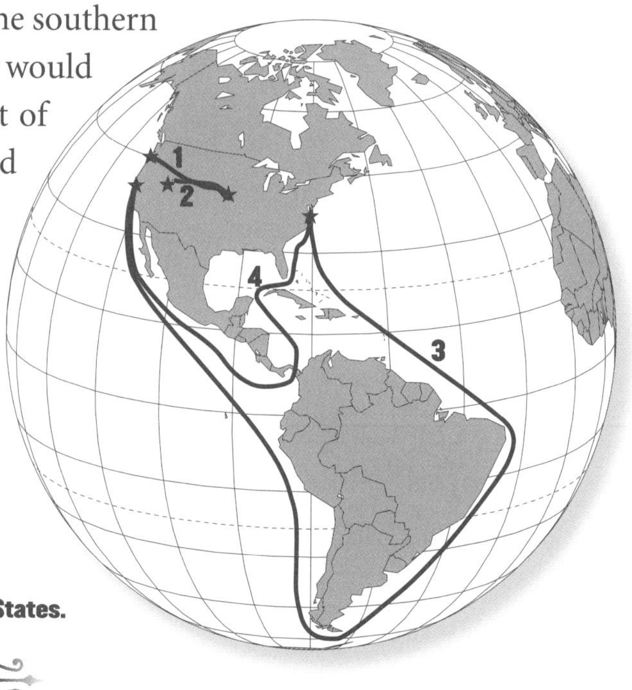

Four of the routes used for western expansion in the United States.

San Francisco in 1851

The cove that served as the marina for ships coming to California was later filled in and is now the heart of San Francisco. It was jam-packed with all sorts of sailing vessels. The most remarkable thing about this crowded cove was that it kept getting more and more crowded, because the officers and crew deserted the ships with the hope of striking it rich in a nearby gold field.

Believe it or not, the number of people who reached California by sea, either by rounding the tip of South America or via Panama equaled the number of people who arrived by land. This is because, until the railroads, sea routes were the only way to move the heaviest and biggest supplies needed by miners who were hoping to strike it rich. The city of San Francisco became very important because it was where the sea route ended.

The trip around the tip of South America to San Francisco was about 18,000 miles long. Not only was it long and boring—the ships were often overcrowded. Even if travelers didn't get seasick themselves, they were surrounded by people who were sick. The food was often rotten, and there was not enough fresh water. The trip could take as little as 4 months and as long as 9 months. It all depended on the weather.

Traveling through Panama was shorter but more expensive and dangerous. Once travelers reached the **Isthmus of Panama**, they had to walk a 75-mile, malaria-infested "land bridge" between South America and North America. The threat of illness was everywhere along this walk through the steamy jungle. Aside from malaria that could be contracted from hordes of mosquitoes, there were poisonous snakes. Diseases like cholera, dysentery, and yellow fever were also very common. Once you made it across Panama you had to wait to be picked up by a ship going north, and sometimes this took a while.

One consequence of the mad rush to California by sea was the development of the clipper ship. These ships were mainly built on the East Coast and were large cargo ships with hulls and rigs designed for speed. Many

Word Round-Up

Isthmus of Panama: The narrow strip of land that lies between the Caribbean Sea and the Pacific Ocean, linking North and South America.

view the clipper ship as the most beautiful American sailing vessel ever built. One clipper ship, the *Flying Cloud*, holds the record for the fastest trip from New York to San Francisco by a commercial sailing vessel. She made the trip in 89 days in 1851.

The Flying Cloud.

Communicating East

Communicating to families Back East was a challenge for pioneers at every stage of their journey—and it didn't get much easier once they'd arrived in the West. Sometimes pioneers heading west on the trail would run into wagon trains going the opposite way, and they would give these eastbound travelers their letters. They hoped the eastbound wagons would leave the letters at the nearest post office in a town or at a trading post. Pioneers traveling west also left letters in "mailboxes" created along the trail, hoping they'd be carried Back East. These mailboxes ranged from piles of rocks or a nook in a cliff wall to a buffalo skull.

The mail system worked very differently back in the pioneer days. The sender didn't pay for the letter to be sent by putting a stamp on it. Rather, the person receiving the letter paid the post office and was charged according to the distance the letter had traveled. A single sheet letter sent over 400 miles would cost the recipient 25 cents. This was a lot to pay when skilled workers earned about 50 cents for working a whole day. Sometimes families would decide on a coded message before they left and write that code on the outside of the letter so their fam-

PONY EXPRESS
St. JOSEPH, MISSOURI to CALIFORNIA
in 10 days or less.

WANTED

YOUNG, SKINNY, WIRY FELLOWS
not over eighteen. Must be expert
riders, willing to risk death daily.
Orphans preferred.
Wages $25 per week.

APPLY, PONY EXPRESS STABLES
St. JOSEPH, MISSOURI

A recruitment flyer for the Pony Express.

DID YOU KNOW?

The Pony Express advertised that it wanted "young men—preferably orphans" for riders because it was very hard and potentially dangerous work. They didn't want the riders to feel the pressure from family about being careful and cautious.

ily member could go to the post office, glance at the code and receive the message without having to pay for the letter. For example, the message, "Aunt Minnie sends her regards" on the outside of the envelope could really mean, "We've arrived safe and sound and will write you more when we get settled." In 1855 the system changed and the sender had to start buying postage stamps, which is like the system we have today.

The Pony Express bridged the gap between the East and West sections during construction of the transcontinental telegraph system.

In those early days of the U.S. Postal Service, a stamp cost just a penny or two to get your letter all the way across the country.

In April 1860, the Pony Express came into being. The Pony Express was an independent mail delivery service that promised letter delivery between California and Missouri in record time. The fastest delivery was 7 days, 17 hours. This was amazing compared to the 5 months it took a wagon train to go that distance. The Pony Express advertised that it wanted young men for riders. Pony Express riders changed horses every 10 to 15 miles and a new rider took over every 70 miles. The Pony Express only lasted until November 1861, when the telegraph services from the East expanded to the West and put them out of business.

The Pony Express

The Pony Express was started by three men who hoped to win the federal mail contract from the Overland Mail company, which guaranteed mail delivery in 20 days from the East Coast to the West Coast. The Pony Express spread 500 horses from St. Joseph, Missouri to San Francisco, California, at 190 stations at approximately 10-mile intervals. Every day riders left the stations at a full gallop—up to 40 riders going in each direction. They'd hop on a fresh horse every 10 miles, and at the end of a 70-mile leg of the journey, one rider would toss the mail-bag to the other. They could get a letter from Missouri to California in about 10 days. It was a fine-tuned, precision operation but it could not compete with either the cost or the speed of the transcontinental telegraph line, which sent its first message across the country on October 24, 1861.

Make Your Own
FRONTIER
POUCH

Many frontiersmen had a leather pouch with them to hold things they wanted to keep safe and dry, like bits of flint for starting fires, or some coins.

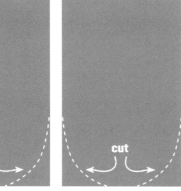

6 inches

9 inches

cut   cut

1 Fold one piece of the 9-by-12-inch felt in half and cut it so you have two pieces that measure 9 by 6 inches. Trim one of the short ends on both 9-by-6-inch pieces so that it's rounded (make sure both pieces match) The pieces should be U-shaped.

SUPPLIES

* 2 pieces of 9-by-12-inch brown-colored felt
* scissors
* ruler
* straight pins
* brown thread
* sewing needle
* hole punch
* 1 foot of leather lacing

2 Take your other piece of felt and cut a 4-by-8-inch piece. This is going to be your fringe. Make narrow, parallel, 3-inch-long cuts every quarter-inch

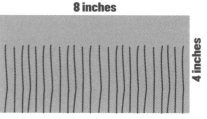

8 inches

4 inches

that are perpendicular to the long side of the piece of felt. Make sure you have about an inch of uncut felt left along the top because you need to sew it onto your pouch.

3 You want the fringe you've made to hang down from the bottom

pin the fringe to the inside of one pouch piece

of your pouch. Place one of your big pouch pieces on a table (it doesn't matter which one). Take your fringe and center it along the bottom curved edge. Pin the edges together so that the fringe is not hanging down but is up against

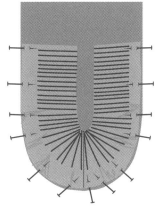

finish pinning the fringe onto one pouch piece

the felt. Now put the other pouch piece on top and pin the whole thing around the three sides—leave the top open. At this point your fringe is on the inside of the pouch.

Sew the pieces together

turn the whole thing right side out (the seam goes on the inside). The fringe should be hanging down.

5 With your hole punch, make a hole about every three-quarters of an inch along the top edge of the pouch. Thread your leather lacing through these holes and make sure you have long enough ends to pull the pouch shut and tie. One way to carry your pouch is to tie it to your belt or even onto your backpack.

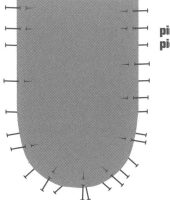

pin the other piece on top

4 Thread your needle and sew the sides of your pouch together where you've pinned it. When you're finished,

turn pouch right side out and make holes and add lace

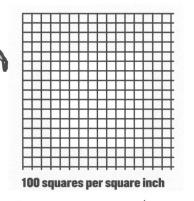

Make Your Own
CROSS-STITCH
SAMPLER

While traveling across the country in a covered wagon, girls learned the alphabet and how to sew at the same time by making cross-stitch samplers. In addition to the alphabet, cross-stitch samplers often had some flowers or birds stitched on and a saying stitched across the bottom. Families kept these samplers for years and today you'll find them in historical societies and museum collections across the country. This project will take a while to complete so don't get discouraged. When you're finished, you'll have your own family heirloom.

Take your graph paper and think about what you want your sampler to look like. Here's where you can plot out your design in pencil. Each stitch is represented by an "X" in a box. Remember that doing a sampler is not only about sewing but about learning the alphabet, so make the letters in the top portion of the sampler. You can design your own letters or use the ones provided. Feel free to put your name centered below the alphabet with the date centered under that. Then think about some kind of decoration you can stitch along the bottom and draw that in. Don't be afraid to make a mistake—that's why you're plotting it out on a piece of graph paper first and that's what erasers are for! If you use graph paper that is set up for 10-count fabric, the design should be exactly the same size as the finished work.

100 squares per square inch

SUPPLIES

* cross-stitch graph paper
* pencil with an eraser
* several different colors of embroidery floss
* embroidery needles
* 10-count cross-stitch fabric
* small embroidery hoop

First, notice that your embroidery floss has six strands to it. Choose a color you want to work with and cut an 18-inch length. Now separate the floss into two threads of three strands each—it's easier to work with the thinner thread. Take one of the three-strand threads and put it aside to use later.

Thread your embroidery needle with your three-strand thread. Pull the end through so that one side of the needle has a 15-inch thread and the other has about 3 inches. Put a knot in the long end of the thread.

3 inches

15 inches

Place your embroidery mesh in your embroidery hoop. It makes the cloth surface easier to work because it pulls it tight—the hoop also gives you something to hold on to when you're working. Using your graph paper design as your guide, start in the upper left hand corner with your "A."

A cross-stitch looks like an "X." It's very important that each X is exactly the same in terms of size and direction. Always cross the X in the same direction throughout the entire sampler. The reason we use embroidery mesh or a fabric with a loose or large weave is because we can use the fabric itself to help us make the stitches even.

looking down on a stitch

Pull the needle through the fabric so that the knot is on the underside of the piece. Look at the weave of the cloth and count one thread over to the left and one thread up and put your needle through. You have one half of your "X." Count one thread down from where you are and bring your needle up through the cloth. Now cross the "X" by counting one thread over to the right and one thread up.

ABCDEFGHI
JKLMNOPQR
STUVWXYZ

THE TRANSCONTINENTAL RAILROAD

A **S THE COUNTRY GREW, THE FEDERAL GOVERNMENT OF** the United States started planning a network of roads, railroad tracks, and canals. Why did the government support these transportation systems? If businesses wanted to sell their goods to more customers they needed to be able to move them from one place to another. Successful businesses would mean more jobs and money for Americans, and this would help make the country better. Roads, canals, and railroads moved people and all kinds of products from the East to the Midwest.

In the 1840s some businessmen tried to get Congress to pay for a railroad that would connect both ends of the country. The idea was popular but the project didn't start for 20 years. They couldn't decide where to lay the tracks! Also, the government wanted to make sure it was possible to run a railroad through the Sierra Nevada and Rocky Mountains before it would give money for the project. Eventually, the businessmen convinced Congress the railroad was possible. The routes were chosen and planning began.

A broadside for the Union Pacific Railroad company.

Two railroad companies formed, called the Union Pacific and the Central Pacific. The huge sums of money needed to help pay for the construction of the railroad came from Congress and private investors. Some of the money was given to the railroad companies and some of it was loaned and had to be paid back. The government also gave the railroads land along the railroad route that the railroad was allowed to sell. Railroad companies began planning out new towns along the proposed routes. They mapped out where things like the town hall and churches would go, and where there would be stores and neighborhoods. Very quickly they printed pamphlets and posters advertising their new towns and the land for sale.

Construction of the **transcontinental railroad** began in 1862. The Central Pacific started in Sacramento, California, heading east. The Union Pacific line began in Omaha, Nebraska, heading west. The Central Pacific ran through the Sierra Nevada, while the Union Pacific went over the Plains and through the Rocky Mountains. When the Union Pacific and Central Pacific started building their railroads, they didn't know exactly where they would meet. They knew the routes they would take, but they were unsure about how fast they would progress. Since the government was paying the railroad lines per mile of track laid, the railroad company that worked fastest would make the most money. In the end, the Union Pacific laid 1,087 miles of track and the Central Pacific covered 690 miles.

Word Round-Up

transcontinental railroad: A railroad that spans all or at least most of the continent. The first transcontinental railroad in the United States was completed in 1869, after track was laid over 1,700 miles (2,700 km) between Sacramento, California, and Omaha, Nebraska.

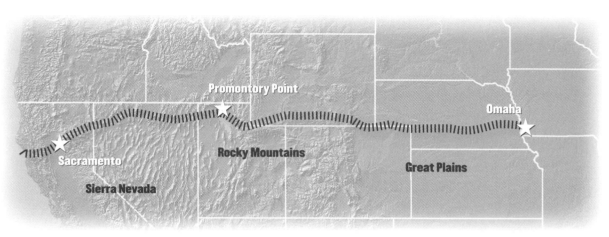

Route of the Transcontinental Railroad.

The Central Pacific hired thousands of Chinese immigrant workers for the dangerous job of blasting through the Sierra Nevada. The workers had to dynamite through rock, and the weather was often terrible. Long sheds over the top of the tracks were built to protect them from heavy snowfalls and avalanches. Hundreds of Chinese workers died during the construction of the Central Pacific line. Those workers who survived settled with their families in their own communities in cities like San Francisco. Today these communities are called "Chinatown." San Francisco's Chinatown is a very important and popular part of the city.

The Union Pacific hired thousands of Irish immigrants as tracklayers. Many Irish had come to America in search of work during the years of the terrible potato famine in Ireland. Like the Chinese immigrants who worked on the Central Pacific line, these Irish workers faced many hardships while laying down miles and miles of tracks. They too had to blast their way through mountains, and build bridges over rivers. They endured the threat of attack by Native Americans. The Union Pacific ran through areas where Native Americans were not happy with the railroad.

⚬⚬ Overheard ⚬⚬

"John Chinaman has broken down the great barrier at last and opened over it the greatest highway yet created for the march of commerce and civilization around the globe."

This report came from the Territorial Enterprise *newspaper in 1868 and was referring to the blasting through the Sierra Nevada.*

Native American Skirmishes

As the track was being laid, hunters were hired by the railroad to kill buffalo in the area as a way to keep the animals away from the tracks. Remember, buffalo were powerful animals and their huge herds could damage the freshly laid tracks. The Native Americans didn't like that the railroad was going through their territory, but when the white hunters began killing their food source, some Native Americans felt like they had to fight back.

On May 10, 1869, the two rail lines met in a great celebration at Promontory, Utah. The owners of the two railroads were there to drive the golden spike into the railroad tie that joined the two lines. At last the two coasts were permanently linked. The connection of the two railroads bridged the 2,000 miles from the

Laying track in Arizona Territory.

West Coast to the Missouri River and served as a great symbolic moment for a country that had just recently been torn apart by the Civil War. Soon railroad lines were built from major northern and southern cities to the transcontinental railroad, connecting the entire country for business and travel.

∞ Overheard ∞

"It is done."

The first message sent to the East and the West coasts by a telegraph operator from Promontory, Utah, when the transcontinental railroad was completed.

The transcontinental railroad changed everything in the movement west. Suddenly, the journey that took 5 months by wagon was just 8 days by train. Four more rail lines quickly crossed the nation. Between 1870 and 1890, millions of people traveled to the West by train, filling in the Great Plains with settlers and homesteaders. Like the pioneers who had traveled by wagon train before them, these pioneers moved for the cheap or free land that was still available throughout the West.

What was cross-country train travel like? While it was a whole lot more comfortable and safe than wagon train, it certainly wasn't very luxurious. Passengers

Joining the tracks for the first transcontinental railroad, Promontory, Utah Territory, 1869.

sat on hard, wooden, straight-backed benches. If the windows were open, hot cinders and smoke from the wood-burning steam engine poured in. If the windows were closed it could be very hot. In 1876 an express train called the Transcontinental Express arrived in San Francisco, just 83 hours and 39 minutes after it left New York City. That's amazing when compared to an overland trip by wagon train that took months and months.

Railroads rapidly changed the face of the West. For one thing, the population of the West exploded. Wherever tracks were laid, communities sprang up. In this respect, railroad companies determined where many of the towns of the nineteenth century would develop. Cities like Kansas City, Topeka, and Albuquerque grew rapidly after railroad tracks were laid through them. Other cities and towns that had once been large or full of action were deserted when railroads were built near other towns. Along with the development of towns, ranches and farms began to dot the prairie.

DID YOU KNOW?

The golden spike that connected the railroads was replaced by an iron one. The original now sits in a museum at Stanford University in California.

What else changed with the railroads? Farmers in the Midwest could ship their crops to market in the East, and goods made in the East could be shipped west. Railroads helped cause the decline of the buffalo because it made it easy for people to rapidly ship buffalo hides and meat to the East before they spoiled. Railroads also shipped cattle from cattle yards to cities like Chicago, which had huge meat-packing plants.

Make Your Own

TRAIN ENGINE

Milk

1 The pint carton is going to be the engineer's "house" at the back of the engine. The round oatmeal box is the rounded part at the front of the engine and the tissue box is the main body of the engine.

Oatmeal

2 Cut the top off the tissue box. You want the oatmeal box to sit halfway down into the tissue box so the front of the engine will be rounded. Put one round end of the oatmeal box up to the end of the tissue box (not the end with the milk carton in it). Trace around the oatmeal box so that there's a half circle traced onto your tissue box. Cut the tissue box on the line you've just made. Don't put the oatmeal box in yet.

cut off top and end

2 inches

SUPPLIES

- pint carton from milk or orange juice, washed, dried, open at the end
- round oatmeal box
- tissue box
- scissors
- pencil
- ruler
- two, 5-inch dowels
- scotch tape
- 4 push pins
- 4 plastic lids off 13-ounce coffee cans
- glue
- five, 2-inch Styrofoam balls
- cardboard toilet paper roll
- Xacto knife
- brown construction paper
- index card
- black marker or aluminum foil

3 To make holes where the axel will go through, measure 2 inches in from each end of the tissue box and ¾ inch up from the bottom—mark and make a hole big enough so that the dowel will move freely.

4 Wrap tape around both ends of each dowel using inch-long pieces of tape. This is to help the dowel move more easily when it turns. Place the dowels through the holes for the axels. When the dowels are in place, put push pins through the center of the coffee can lids and push them into the ends of the dowels to make the wheels.

5 Place glue on the bottom of each of the Styrofoam balls and put two of them in the end of the tissue box that will hold the engineer's house. Place the other three between the two axels. These balls will allow the oatmeal box and milk carton to sit high enough in the tissue box.

6 Put the oatmeal box and the milk carton in place. One end of the oatmeal box should be sticking out the end of the tissue box by about an inch. Take the toilet paper tube and hold it in place on the oatmeal box where you think the smokestack should go (maybe 2 inches back from the front of the engine). Trace around the bottom of the tube with your marker onto the oatmeal box. VERY CAREFULLY cut out the opening for the tube with your Xacto knife. Cut on the inside of the line to make it a little smaller than the tube so that the tube fits snugly in the hole.

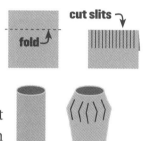

7 Cut a piece of construction paper that measures 5 inches by 5½ inches for the smokestack. Measure two inches down the long sides and fold. Make a series of straight line cuts perpendicular to the fold every half inch that measure about 1½ inches long. Unfold and wrap the paper around the cardboard tube placing the folded end toward the top of the stack. Scrunch it down to come level with the top of the tube and tape to the cardboard.

This gives the smokestack that characteristic flared shape.

8 Cut another piece of construction paper to 4½ inches by 5½ inches and tape it to both sides of the open milk carton. The paper will curve like the oatmeal box. This makes the roof over the engineer's house.

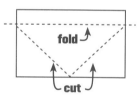

9 Finally, make your cowcatcher. This is what would literally push animals off the track at the front of the train. Take the index card and make a fold about a half-inch down on the long edge. Measure and mark the middle of the index card on the other long side. Cut from the fold to the middle point making a big triangle. Put tape above the fold and tape it to the bottom front of the engine on the tissue box under the oatmeal box so that it hangs down in front.

10 If you want to decorate your train, you could use aluminum foil to make it look metallic, paint, or magic markers.

front view

cowcatcher in place

BUILDING HOMES

HEN A WAGON TRAIN REACHED THE END OF the trail, the pioneers were exhausted from their long journey. Still, they had to build something to live in right away. How did they decide where to build their house? Sometimes it was as easy as stumbling across a nice piece of land and claiming it at the nearest "claims" office. According to the Homestead Act, as long as a pioneer planned to live and work on the land for at least 5 years, the land would become theirs as long as they didn't abandon it. What did pioneers consider a nice piece of land? Land that they could farm. They looked for land that had good soil for planting, and was clear of trees and near a source of water.

A homesteader turning sod on his claim in North Dakota.

The hardest part was building a house. This job was a little easier in the Pacific Northwest, where there were many trees, than it was out on the prairie where trees were scarce. On the prairie, many families had to build homes out of something other than wood. Some of the first homes pioneers made on the prairie looked like caves. They were just holes dug out of a hill. The front of these hill homes usually had only two openings—one for a window and one for a door. Usually pioneers lived in these homes only until they could build something better. Since they couldn't afford to buy wood and transport it over the long distances, they ended up building houses out of earth.

Soddies

Prairie earth, or sod, is held so tightly together by the roots of the thick prairie grasses that it can be used like bricks. To build a sod house, or a **soddie**, as the pioneers called them, pioneers cut "bricks" out of the sod. The bricks measured about 2 feet by 1 foot by 4 inches. Pioneers found a flat piece of ground, usually on top of a small hill, and used that as the place to build their house. They would decide on the size and shape of the house. Then the settlers would begin cutting and stacking bricks. They made the walls two or three bricks thick, with the grass side laid down. The roots quickly intertwined, locking the bricks together.

A sod house.

As the settlers worked, they left holes for windows and doors. When they first built their soddies, settlers used greased paper to let in light and a buffalo hide as a door. Later they filled the holes with pre-made glass windows and wooden doors. Pioneers framed the ceilings of their soddies with whatever wood they had. Some of the wood might have come from their wagon. Once this support was in place, they laid **tarpaper** over the wood frame and topped the tarpaper with more sod.

The first home of the early pioneer on a homestead near Meadow, South Dakota.

Living in a sod house had its unpleasant moments. When it rained, the roof would get wet and leak for days, sometimes even after the rain had stopped. Settlers put up stretched muslin (cotton cloth) as a "ceiling," to catch whatever fell from the tarpaper when it wasn't raining. Centipedes, ants, mice, and snakes were frequent uninvited guests. Soddies were quite dark, but pioneers whitewashed the inside walls to lighten up the interior.

There were also good things about sod houses. Since they used cow chip or buffalo chip–burning stoves for cooking, they just had to poke a hole in the roof for the stovepipe. The thick outer walls were a benefit because they provided great insulation and kept soddies warm in winter and cool in summer.

Very few soddies remain standing today. Old soddies dotted the prairie for years after they were abandoned by settlers who built more permanent houses. They were often the only upright structures for miles around. Over time, however, most of the soddies collapsed and eventually disappeared back into the earth.

⌒ Overheard: Laura Ingalls Wilder ⌒

"There was a small greased-paper window beside the door. But the wall was so thick that the light from the window stayed near the door. That front wall was built of sod. Mr. Hanson had dug out his house, and then he had cut long strips of prairie sod and laid them on top of one another, to make the front wall. It was a good, thick wall with not one crack in it. No cold could get through that wall . . . the ceiling was made of hay. Willow boughs had been laid across and their branches woven together, but here and there the hay that had been spread on them showed through."

On the Banks of Plum Creek

❧ Overheard: Mattie Oblinger ❧

"At home in our house and a sod at that! . . . It is not quite so convenient as a nice frame, but I would as soon live in it as the cabins I have lived in. The only objection I have is that we have no floor yet."

In a letter from Nebraska written in 1873

Log Cabins

If a pioneer family settled in a land with lots of trees, they raced to clear the land and build a cabin before the chill of autumn turned to the snow of winter. The result was a simple yet sturdy structure called a log cabin.

All along the American frontier, pioneers built log cabins wherever there was wood available. Log cabin–style homes were first built by Swedish colonists who settled in Delaware in 1638, but later became the symbol of westward expansion. After choosing a farm site with good soil and water, a pioneer family cleared the trees from their land. They picked out the straightest logs and cut notches near the ends of them to make joints. The size of the cabin depended on the length of the logs. The pioneers stacked the logs in

A sturdy log cabin.

a rectangle shape on the ground. They joined them at the corners and filled in the cracks between the logs with mud and moss to keep out the wind and cold.

A log cabin long abandoned.

Pioneers cut a few spaces for windows and a wooden door that they attached with leather hinges. The windows were often made of paper covered in grease, making them somewhat see-through. They made the roof by overlapping long pieces of clapboard to keep out the rain and snow. Finally, they built a fireplace and chimney of stone.

Loneliness

After the pioneers had built their homes and finally had a moment to relax and take a deep breath, many of them were hit by loneliness. Many pioneers had left family, friends, and communities they loved very much. Now they found themselves alone in a new place.

Sometimes the nearest neighbor was tens or even hundreds of miles away, making it very hard or even impossible to visit. Pioneers had to walk, ride a horse, or hitch up a horse to a wagon in order to go visiting, and sometimes it took days to get where they were going. Some pioneers felt a kind of loneliness we can only imagine.

Life in a log cabin was difficult. It was very hard to keep them clean. Floors were either dirt or covered with **puncheons.** These were logs cut in half the long way. The almost-windowless houses were dark and dreary. Since log cabins usually were built as temporary structures, settlers thought they would build a log cabin to live in just for the first year or so, and then build something better. But many pioneers stayed in their log cabins for a long time. They improved their cabins by putting in glass windows, and building new rooms and even second floors.

Later, as farms prospered and frontier settlements gained stability, the settlers often built more permanent houses. As log cabins became less common, they became symbols of poverty and common sense. U.S. Presidents Abraham Lincoln, Ulysses S. Grant, William Henry Harrison, and James Garfield all claimed to have been born in log cabins as part of their election campaigns. This was a way for them to show that they came from common folk and had common sense.

Word
Round-Up

soddie: A home made of sod- or earth-bricks stacked together.

tarpaper: A heavy paper coated with tar, often used as a roof because it was relatively waterproof.

puncheons: The flat side of logs cut in half the long way, often laid together for floors.

∞ Overheard: Anne Bingham ∞

"In all the years spent there we never could see a neighbor's light in the evening. I did wish so much we could, to relieve the aloneness."

Written about their farm near Junction City, Kansas

Make Your Own
SOD HOUSE

cut brownies into 1-inch-by-1-inch squares

cut squares in half

1 Prepare the brownies according to the recipe and bake them in a large, rectangular 13-by-9-inch pan. When they're cooled completely cut them into 1-inch squares. Use a plastic knife because it makes a clean cut through brownies.

chocolate frosting

cut brownie in half for edge of door

2 Think about how bricks are laid—they overlap on every other row. Cut your 1-inch brownie squares in half. Lay a row of brownie bricks in a 6½-inch square. You might want to draw a 6½-inch square on your cardboard so you have a guideline. You can take each brick and make it more solid by squishing each of the sides with your fingers. Leave an opening of about 1 inch in the front for a door.

3 Spread chocolate frosting on the top of each layer of bricks to act as your mortar for the next layer. You might have to use your fingers to help spread the frosting. Lay your next layer of brownie bricks being aware that you want to overlap where the bricks come together on the previous layer. Spread more frosting. Repeat this process until you have five layers of brick brownies. End with a final layer of frosting.

pretzel rod roof

4 The pretzel rods are for your roof. Place them side by side so that they're running parallel to the side with the door opening.

5 To finish your brownie soddie, you're going to "plant" some grass on the roof. Take a small bowl and mix several

SUPPLIES

* brownie mix
* plastic knife
* piece of stiff cardboard for the base
* pencil & ruler
* ready-made frosting (chocolate)
* about a dozen 7-inch pretzel rods
* green food coloring
* water
* shredded coconut

drops of green food coloring in about a cup of water. Now put a handful of coconut in the water, swirl it around, then drain off the water and dump the green coconut onto a piece of paper towel to dry. When dry, spread a thin layer of frosting on your pretzel roof and sprinkle your "grass" on to the roof.

Make Your Own
LOG CABIN

1 Spread newspaper out on a table so you have a nice workspace and don't make a mess. Place your piece of cardboard in the middle of your workspace.

2 Take 20 pretzel rods out of the bag and bite an inch off of both ends of 10 of them. Make sure you have plenty of water in case your mouth gets dry. Take your time—don't rush and get any pretzel down the wrong pipe.

SUPPLIES

* newspaper
* a piece of stiff cardboard
* a package of pretzel rods
* a box of graham crackers
* chocolate cake frosting
* 8½-by-11-inch piece of brown cardstock
* Multi-Bran Chex cereal

3 On your workspace, arrange your pretzel rods next to each other, alternating between pretzels you've bitten the ends off of and pretzels you haven't bitten the ends off of. Then, separate the pretzel rods into four groups of five. (Two of these groups should have two bitten pretzels and three non-bitten pretzels, and the other two groups should have three bitten and two non-bitten.)

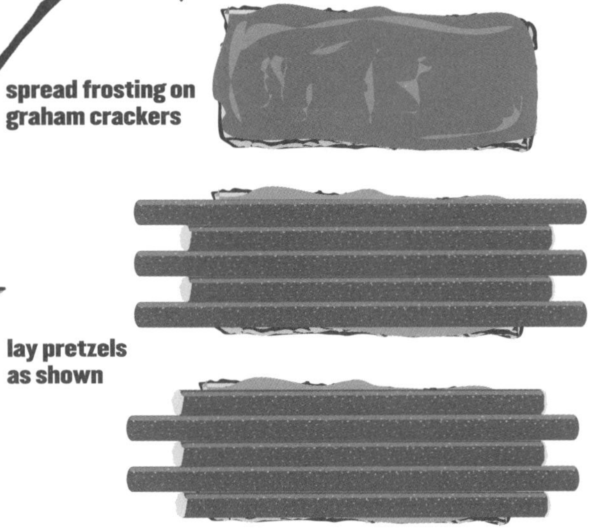

spread frosting on graham crackers

lay pretzels as shown

4. Lay four graham crackers on the table. Spread a thick coating of cake frosting on each of them. Then place five pretzel rods lengthwise onto each coated cracker—they should stick well to the frosting. Again, as you lay the rods, alternate between bitten and non-bitten pretzels. When you're done you will have four log cabin walls.

5. On top of your cardboard, slide the walls together as pictured below. Use more frosting on the inside of your cabin if you need to make the walls sturdier. You now have four standing walls.

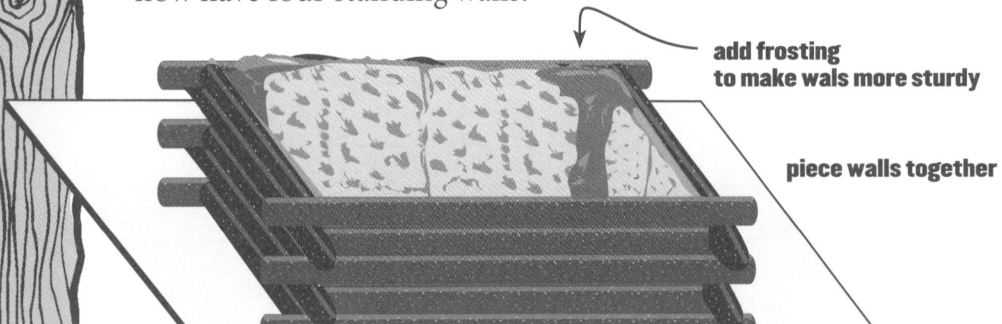

6. Fold your cardstock in half widthwise and then coat it with a thin layer of frosting. This will be your roof, and you can add "shingles" to it by sticking pieces of Chex cereal into the frosting. If necessary, add a little bit of frosting to each "shingle" to make it stick.

7. Take a long look at your cabin, or even take a picture of it, before you eat the walls. But only eat the cabin with a parent's permission—and whatever you do, don't eat the cardboard roof!

add frosting to make wals more sturdy

piece walls together

FRONTIER FARMING AND FOOD

THE FIRST YEAR OF LIFE AS A HOMESTEADER WAS very difficult. After making the long journey in a covered wagon pioneers were absolutely exhausted, but they still had a lot of work to do. There were no stores where pioneers could buy groceries or supplies, so whatever they needed, they had to find in nature or make for themselves. First the pioneers cleared an area of land and built a house of some kind. If pioneers decided to settle in the Northwest or California, in the first 3 years a pioneer would clear about 22 acres of woods for farmland. That work

Clearing the land was back-breaking work for settlers.

Bee

This kind of bee doesn't have wings or sting. This kind of bee is a group of people that gather together to help out a family. Families organized work bees at different farms, so that everyone who participated in a bee would eventually benefit from one. It was common for frontier people to gather in bees to clear land, build a house or barn, or harvest the crops. Women provided the food at these work bees, but they also participated in bees of their own. When a woman was getting married or having a baby, the women in her community held a quilting bee, where they would gather to make a quilt. These were social events. Another type of bee was called a husking bee. These events were usually held in a barn where the host had divided a huge amount of corn into two equal piles. The huskers would divide into two groups and race each other to see who could finish husking their pile of corn first! If a young man found a red ear of corn, he got to kiss any young lady he chose. Today, people still have barn-raisings or quilting bees in many parts of the country.

included cutting trees, clearing bushes and vines, and pulling the stumps. Clearing the land was so hard that pioneer families would often get together to do the work as a group, which they called a bee.

Pioneer families tried to have their fields and farms ready for planting by the first spring after their arrival in the West. It was important to plant as soon as the ground dried out from the winter so that the crops could grow as large as possible. Pioneers often planted potatoes first because potatoes didn't need a perfectly plowed field to grow. They could even plant potatoes around tree stumps that the farmer had not pulled out yet.

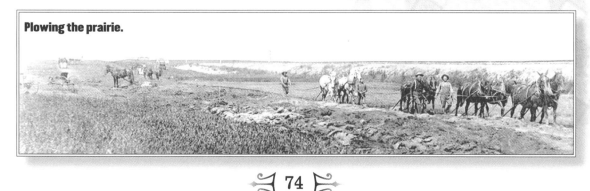

Plowing the prairie.

John Deere

In 1837, John Deere designed the first cast-steel plow that would change the life of the prairie farmer. The plow was made of wrought iron and had a steel share that could cut through sticky prairie soil without clogging. By 1855, John Deere's factory was selling over 10,000 steel plows a year. John Deere became a millionaire.

Working in the fields was back-breaking work that began before sunup and lasted until sundown. To grow crops like wheat, barley, and corn, the farmer had to plow the fields. In some areas of the Great Plains this was virtually impossible without a steel plow. The sod was so thick with roots that it was difficult to churn up. Before the steel plow was widely available, settlers broke the sod any way they could—sometimes they even chopped the sod with an axe! During planting and harvesting time everyone in the family worked in the fields. At other times of the year, mothers and daughters did household chores like cooking, cleaning, making butter, mending, and sewing, and only the father and sons worked outdoors. After the crop seeds were planted, pioneers had to battle the birds who liked to eat them. It was usually the children's job to try to keep the birds away by chasing them and yelling and screaming.

Times of extreme dry weather, also known as drought, happened off and on periodically throughout the 1880s and 1890s. The crops withered in the field as the prairie soil turned to dust. Fierce winds whipped up dangerous dust storms. With so much dirt swirling in the air, sometimes the settlers couldn't see to their barn from their houses. Pioneers found that the fine dust got into everything. It worked its way into houses, down chimneys, and through cracks in the walls. Another danger during dry weather was prairie fires, which were often started by lightning. They were impossible to control and everything a family owned could be turned to a pile of smoking ash

Word Round-Up

staple: Something that is used by most people on a regular basis, like sugar and salt.

tenderize: To make meat tender through cooking or marinating.

in a matter of minutes. Then there were the grasshoppers and locusts that sometimes swarmed through the prairie. They ate everything in their path and left crops stripped of their leaves and seeds.

Pioneers had to grow most of what they ate. Even if they didn't have large farms, families planted big gardens and grew vegetables like beans, peas, squash, pumpkins, turnips, cabbage, potatoes, beets, and anything else they might like. They also planted apple or pear orchards so that they could have both fresh and dried fruit.

The job of cutting up and hanging the fruit and vegetables out to dry for use during the long winter months usually fell to the women. One of the most time-consuming jobs was cutting fresh corn from the cobs to dry. The dried corn would eventually be ground into grits or cornmeal, then used to make johnnycakes or mush. The frontier family diet was pretty boring—especially in the winter when they had to rely on what they had dried or salted the previous season. **Staples** like coffee, tea, sugar, and wheat flour had to be bought at a store, which was often so far away that it took days on end to get there and back. So these things were used sparingly.

Over time, many of the pioneers who settled on the Great Plains became farmers who specialized in growing corn and wheat. As agricultural technology improved and access to markets in every direction became easier due to the railroads, farms got bigger and bigger. The amazing thing is that some of the largest farms began with a single frustrated pioneer family trying to "bust the sod" in order to plant enough crops to survive.

Meat and Dairy

Pioneers usually had a couple of pigs, some chickens, and a milk cow to provide milk and cream to make butter. Pork was prepared in a variety of ways. It was either eaten fresh, or salted and cured for bacon, ham, or pork shoulders. Wild game like deer, duck, bear, and partridge usually ended up in the stew pot with vegetables. This would **tenderize** the meat by long cooking.

Grow Your Own
ROOT VEGETABLES

Today, many people have no idea where their food comes from. The pioneers certainly did, because it came from their own hard work! They gathered, killed, or grew everything they ate. This project will give you an idea of where some of your vegetables come from.

1 Put four or five toothpicks into the sides of the potato and place this on your glass of water, making sure an eye is in the water. An eye is an indentation in your potato where the roots grow from. The toothpicks will keep the potato from slipping down into the glass.

2 Do the same with the carrot. Carrots also have teeny-tiny eyes—you'll be able to see them if you look closely. Cut your carrot into sections, put the toothpicks in, and suspend them in a glass of water.

3 After a couple of days, you'll notice that some roots will be growing out of the eyes in the vegetables. Make sure to keep the glasses filled with water. When the roots look long and healthy, plant them in your clay pots, making sure the root systems are down in the dirt and fully covered. Remember, these are root vegetables so you need to make sure the pot is big enough to accommodate the potatoes and carrots growing beneath the surface. Place your pots in a sunny window. Make sure they get plenty of water and watch your vegetables grow.

SUPPLIES

* toothpicks
* a small red potato
* several small glasses of water
* carrots with part of the green tops still attached (baby carrots don't work)
* paring knife
* large clay pots
* potting soil

Make Your Own

JOHNNYCAKES

Johnnycakes were kind of the "fast food" for pioneers.

1 Combine cornmeal, salt, butter, and sugar in the mixing bowl. Add the boiling water. Add the milk and mix thoroughly to make a smooth thick batter. If it gets too thick you can add a little warm water.

2 Spread a light coating of oil on the griddle or frying pan. Heat the pan on medium-high heat so that when you put a drop of water on the surface, it bounces. Then reduce the heat to medium.

3 Place the batter by spoonfuls onto the hot pan, like pancake batter. You don't want the johnnycakes to be more than about a half-inch thick. Cook for about 5 minutes on each side. The johnnycakes should be crisp and slightly brown when done. Serve the johnnycakes hot with butter and maple syrup.

SUPPLIES

* 1 cup of cornmeal (preferably white)
* 1 teaspoon salt
* 1 tablespoon butter
* 1 tablespoon sugar
* mixing bowl
* spoon
* 1 cup boiling water
* ½ cup milk
* griddle or frying pan
* cooking oil
* spatula
* maple syrup & butter

Make Your Own

STRAW HAT

Men and boys wore straw hats in the fields and out on the trail. Here, we'll make a modern version of the straw hat.

1 If you're using brown paper bags, cut the bag from top to bottom along one fold and then cut the bottom out. You'll be left with one long piece of brown paper. Trace three circles, 14 inches in diameter, on your kraft paper or brown paper bag.

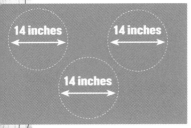

14 inches

14 inches

14 inches

2 Cut out the three circles. Take one and wet the middle of it with water. Don't get it soaking wet. If there's writing on your paper, make sure you're getting the side with the writing on it wet.

3 Turn one of the smaller bowls upside down on a table. Mold the wet circle to the outside of the bowl. This makes the part that will fit your head, called the crown. You should have an inch or two of extra paper all the way around the bowl. Make creases in the extra paper to help it lay flat on the table. This will be for the brim of your hat. Put the other bowl on top of your paper to hold the shape, and let it dry completely (this might take an hour or more).

bowl

crown

bowl

4 When the hat crown is dry, take the bottom bowl and place it in the middle of the two remaining circles. Trace around the edge and cut out the circles. These are for the outside part for the brim.

glue side down

glue side up

brim →

crown

brim ↙

5 Place a line of glue all the way around one of the outside circles and then put the crown down on the brim. Put a line of glue on the other brim piece and put it down over the crown. Wrap the twine around the base of the crown as a kind of decoration. You can wrap as many rows as you like, running a line of glue underneath to hold it in place.

SUPPLIES

* kraft paper from a craft store or a couple of brown paper bags
* scissors
* a round bowl roughly 14 inches in diameter
* pencil
* water
* 2 smaller bowls that will fit on your head
* Elmer's glue
* twine

Make Your Own

PRAIRIE SUNBONNET

Women and girls wore sunbonnets anytime they went outside because, unlike today, women prized fair skin. There are several different styles of sunbonnet. The one you'll make is the type that would most likely have been worn along the trail.

7 inches
4½ inches
22 inches

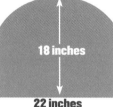

18 inches
11 inches
22 inches

to make TWO copies of the brim so make sure the fabric is doubled when pinning the brim. You'll only need one back piece. You'll have a total of three cut pieces when you're done with this step.

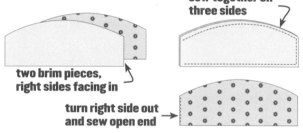

sew together on three sides

two brim pieces, right sides facing in

turn right side out and sew open end

1. First you have to make a pattern. On your kraft paper, measure and draw your brim—there should be a straight edge 22 inches long, two sides 4½ inches long perpendicular to the long edge, and for the final side you should draw a gentle arc with the widest part measuring 7 inches. Now measure and draw the back of the bonnet. Again, you need a 22-inch-long straight edge, but the two sides perpendicular to the long side will measure 11 inches. Again, make a gentle arc with the widest part measuring 18 inches.

2. Cut out your patterns and pin them to your fabric. You need

SUPPLIES

kraft paper for making a pattern

pencil

ruler

scissors

1½ yards of at least 45-inch-wide muslin or cotton fabric

straight pins

sewing needle (or sewing machine)

thread

iron

1 yard grosgrain ribbon (about 1 inch wide)

3. Take the paper pattern off the brim pieces and pin the two pieces together with the RIGHT sides in. Sew all the sides together except for one of the short sides, making your stitches a half-inch from the edges. Turn the brim piece right-side-out and iron the seams flat. Sew the open end shut and iron that seam too. Set aside.

4 Make a half-inch hem around three sides of the back of your bonnet piece (you don't have to hem the long straight side). Pin the straight edge of the back to the straight edge of the brim making sure you put RIGHT sides together. Sew these pieces together and iron all the hemmed edges. Iron the seam toward the back of the bonnet.

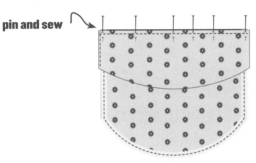

pin and sew

5 Put the sunbonnet wrong side up flat on a table. Measure 9 inches down each side of the bonnet back and mark, with a pin, a spot two inches in.

2 inches in

9 inches

basting stitch

2 inches in

Between the two pins, draw a gentle arc that matches the arc of the bonnet back. Take a needle and thread and with long stitches called basting stitches, sew along that line. Before you tie the end, pull the thread so that the bonnet back gathers and put your bonnet on your head and make the gathered part very loosely fit the bottom of your head. You can ask someone to help you with this part. Now tie a good strong knot. If you want to, you can leave the gathers loose or sew over this section to keep the gathers in place. You can take a piece of your grosgrain ribbon and sew it over the gathered spot as a kind of decoration.

6 Finally, measure two equal lengths of the ribbon—it's up to you how long—and sew them on to the sides of the brim for your ties.

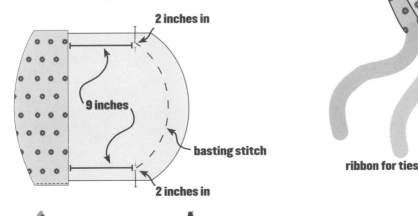

gathered part

ribbon for ties

AT HOME AND AT SCHOOL

MANY FRONTIER FAMILIES DIDN'T PACK HOUSEHOLD items for the journey west. Sometimes, along the way, families had to toss what they did bring to lighten the load for their oxen. That meant the pioneers often had to make household items once they reached the end of the trail. This involved carving bowls and utensils out of wood—or shaping them with clay gathered from the bed of a creek. Pioneers made candles from **tallow** and beeswax, soap from **lye** and tallow, furniture from pieces of the wagon, and blankets and cloth from sheep's wool.

Different types and shapes of pottery and crocks.

Sewing and Sheep

Many pioneers had a few sheep or knew people who owned sheep, so wool was available. Every pioneer girl knew how to card and spin wool into yarn, which they then dyed different colors. The pioneers made dyes out of things they found in the forest or on the prairie. Walnuts and onion skins made brown dye. Goldenrod blossoms made light yellow. Queen Anne's lace blossoms made light green, while blueberries made blue. Usually the colors from homemade dye were not very bright, but they gave the wool some color.

A woman spinning yarn on a spinning wheel.

Once a family settled Out West, the women and girls made most of their blankets and clothes. Remember, many girls had learned to sew while on the trail by practicing sewing the alphabet on cross-stitch samplers. As clothes got too worn out to wear or repair, they were cut up, and the pieces were used for quilts or braided rugs. Many women sewed quilts that were fancy and beautiful, and showed off the pioneer women's artistic talent. Braided rugs covered frontier floors. They were both warm and colorful.

A braided rug.

Making Soap

About once a year pioneers made soap. They saved the ashes from their fires every day in a big barrel. When the barrel was full, the pioneers poured in rainwater. The dissolved ashes made lye. The pioneers then mixed the lye with **lard**, **drippings**, and leftover candle wax in a huge pot and brought this mixture to a boil. Eventually, it would thicken and turn into a jelly-like soap that the pioneers poured into stone crocks. Pioneer women used scoopfuls of this soap as detergent in boiling pots of clothes. Generally, one barrel of ashes mixed with 12 pounds of fat made 40 pounds of soap, which lasted about a year.

Frontier School

When children weren't helping out at the homestead, either in the fields or indoors, they went to school—if one existed, that is. Pioneers did two things to create a "community" when enough of them had settled in one spot. First they built a church, and then they built a school. Once a school building was in place the parents hired a teacher. The pay for teachers was very low out on the frontier. Teachers earned about 75¢ to $1 dollar per 3-month term, plus 50¢ per student. Often the teacher lived with the families of their students on a rotating basis so that room and board became part of their pay. Sometimes there was so little money in a frontier community that a teacher was paid with sacks of grain.

A pioneer school.

Not surprisingly, it was tough to get teachers, particularly good ones, to work in a frontier school. Most teachers were men. There were times when frontier teachers weren't much older (or wiser) than their students. Frontier schools didn't require that teachers have a college education in order to teach. All the students sat in one room and shared what few books, slates, and slate pencils the school had. School was only in session when the kids weren't needed to help in the fields. This meant the highest attendance was in the winter when there was little outdoor work to do on the farm.

Discipline was harsh. In those days no one had to go to school and a teacher could discipline students any way he wanted. When children misbehaved, the teacher would often whip them with a stick. The teacher had to demonstrate his authority or potentially lose the respect of the rest of the class.

What did children learn? Sometimes only the basics, like arithmetic and how to read. Frontier children usually attended school until they were about 12 years old, although a few students stayed on in hopes of learning enough to do well on a college entrance exam.

Word Round-Up

tallow: Melted animal fat used for making candles and soap.

lye: Ashes dissolved in water.

lard: A soft white solid fat from hogs.

drippings: Fat and juices from cooking meat.

Make Your Own
FOUR-PATCH BLOCK QUILT

These beautiful pieced blankets kept the pioneers warm. They were also wonderful, creative designs made with scrap material. If you ever have a chance, go to a quilt show, which often features old and new quilts.

Your quilt will contain four blocks when it is complete. Here are directions to make one block, so you'll have to repeat this four times.

1 Measure and cut out a square of paper that is 5½ inches on all sides. This is your pattern. Use the pattern to cut out eight squares of the light fabric and eight squares of the dark fabric. Place one light square on top of one dark square with the right sides of the fabric facing each other. Pin these together and sew along one edge. Use a quarter-inch seam. Repeat this seven more times. Iron the seams to one side.

2 Put two of these units together with the right sides facing each other so that opposites are across from each other. It should look like a checkerboard. Pin these units along one edge, then sew this seam together.

10½ inches
10½ inches

Open and press with the iron to flatten the seam. Repeat this three more times. A block should measure 10½ inches. Iron all seams flat.

3 Pin two blocks together with the right sides facing each other and light and dark squares opposite each other. Sew along that edge. Repeat this step for the other two blocks. Finally, sew the two halves to each other. Iron the seams flat.

other block design options

SUPPLIES

- piece of paper to make a pattern
- ruler
- scissors
- 1 yard of four different cotton fabrics (make sure they go together and that two of them are basically light and two are basically dark)
- pins
- sewing machine or needle and thread
- iron and ironing board
- 1 yard of cotton fabric for quilt backing
- 1 yard of low-loft polyester batting
- embroidery floss and large needle

To make the borders, chose one fabric and cut two strips 2½ inches wide and 20½ inches long for the top and bottom inner borders. Pin the strips (with right sides facing) to the top and bottom of your square and sew these seams. Cut two more strips out of the same fabric measuring 2½ inches wide by 24½ inches long. Pin and sew these on the side inner borders. Iron flat.

finished quilt top

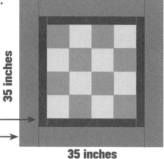

35 inches

inner border →

outer border →

35 inches

For an outer border, chose another fabric and cut two strips 5½ inches wide by 24½ inches long. Sew these on the top and bottom of the quilt. Cut two more strips, 5½ inches wide by 34½ inches long and sew on the side outer borders. Iron flat. Congratulations! You've just made a quilt top.

Your quilt top should measure about 35 inches by 35 inches. Lay your fabric for the quilt backing on the floor or a table top and place your quilt top on top.

quilt top—WRONG SIDE UP

batting

Cut the backing about the same size as the quilt top. Do the same thing for the polyester batting.

To finish off your quilt, place your batting on a smooth surface. Now place the backing on top of the batting making sure the right side is up. Finally, place the quilt top on top of the backing fabric WRONG SIDE UP.

Pin around the edges to secure the layers. Stitch around the edge, making sure to sew through all three layers. Leave a 12-inch opening on one side. Trim the corners. Turn the quilt right side out through this opening. Hand stitch the opening closed with tiny stitches. Then stitch about a half-inch from the edge all the way around your quilt with your sewing machine or by hand.

turn quilt right side out

You might want to tie your quilt at each corner where blocks meet. This would give you about 13 ties (the corners plus a knot at the center of each block), but this is up to you. To tie your quilt, thread your large needle with embroidery thread and push the needle from the top

backing—RIGHT SIDE UP

quilt top—WRONG SIDE UP

backing— RIGHT SIDE UP

batting

sew around edges

leave opening

down through the three layers then back up to the top. Leave about a 3-inch tail on top and cut the thread to match the tail. Tie the knot like you would tie your shoelaces, then double knot it. Trim the thread tails so they're about 1½ inches long.

tie quilt at the corners and center of each block

Make Your Own

BRAIDED RUG

The pioneers used old scraps of cloth for their braided rugs.

1 Find a nice flat surface to work on, like a table or the floor. Then cut your wool into strips 1¾ inches wide. If you cut across the grain it will prevent the fabric from fraying. Sew all the strips of one color together so you end up with a really long strip. Make the seams at a 45-degree angle to make them stronger.

45° seam when sewing strips together

2 Once you have your strips sewn together set up your iron and ironing board. You want to make a "roll" out of the cloth by folding one edge over and the other one overlapping it. It might help to fold over a long section and pin the edges before ironing them flat. After a while, you'll get the hang of what you're doing and you won't need to pin the fabric.

long strips of cloth

side view of strip—make a roll by folding one edge back and then overlapping with the other edge

SUPPLIES

* **1 yard of light-weight wool in 3 different colors (or any cloth you have around the house like old T-shirts, but just make sure all the cloth is of similar weight so that your braid and your rug are even)**
* **good scissors**
* **sewing machine or needle and thread**
* **iron and ironing board**
* **straight pins**
* **3 rubber bands**
* **big needle and heavy-duty (tapestry) thread**

3 strips of cloth to braid

next bring M over R—repeat the pattern starting with L over M

3 You should end up with three very long ironed strips. Now start at the end of one strip and start folding it over—make the first fold at about 3 inches and keep folding the material over and over. When you have about a foot left, place a rubber band around the roll to keep it from coming undone. Repeat this with all three different colored strips. Sew the ends of the three colors together and you're ready to being braiding!

4 As you braid you might want to hook the strip to the back of a chair so that you can pull it taut. Make your braid fairly tight and make sure it's even. Now you see why you want to have the three rolls of color. Let more of each color out of the rubber band roll as necessary.

5 Once you have the strips braided together it's time to sew your rug with your big needle and heavy-duty thread. On a flat surface take one end of your braid and begin to make a coil, keeping the braid as flat as possible. Sew the coil together as you go, making your stitches as close to the edge as possible. This is a little tough to do with the center coils so ask someone to help. As the rug gets bigger, it becomes easier to sew the braid.

sew together

Make a coil and sew the coil together by pushing the needle up from the bottom and making Xs (if you can). You can just do an overhand stitch if you can't do the Xs.

to braid—bring back strip L to the front and over the middle strip M—then bring R over L

Make Your Own
HAND-DIPPED CANDLES

Candles were absolutely essential on the frontier. The only light in a room came from a fire in the fireplace and from oil lanterns or candles. Lamp oil (often whale oil) was not easy to come by, so pioneer families relied on candles for light. Pioneer women and children made candles by pouring molten wax into pewter candle molds brought from home, or by dipping a wick over and over again into the wax. Here are instructions for the dipping method.

Ask an adult for help and permission before you do this project because it involves boiling water.

1 Fill the pot about half full with water and put it on the stove top. Bring the water to a boil, then turn the burner down so that the water just simmers.

2 Put some paraffin or candle wax in the coffee can and melt it by placing the can in the pot of simmering water. Do not place the coffee can directly on a burner or open flame. As the wax melts add more, and as that melts add more again. You can color it by adding bits of crayon. Use your chopstick or dowel to stir the color into the wax. If you have 6 inches of wax in your can, that is how long your candles can be.

3 Cut a 15-inch piece of candle wick and tie one end around the middle of a wooden spoon. Try to straighten the wick as much as possible. If you're dipping several candles, repeat this step.

SUPPLIES

* large pot for boiling water
* paraffin or candle wax or old crayons (paraffin is easy to find in a grocery store and candle wax can be bought in a craft store)
* empty coffee can (the taller the can, the longer your candles will be)
* crayon
* a chopstick or dowel
* candle wick
* scissors
* several long wooden spoons
* 2 chairs
* newspaper

4 Place the two chairs back to back several inches apart. Lay newspaper on the floor beneath the space between the chairs. When the wax has melted to liquid, dip each wick into the wax so it coats the wick. Pull it out and place the two ends of the spoon onto the chairs (over the newspaper) to cool. While this is cooling, dip your other candles and put them on the chairs as well.

5 Let the wax cool completely before dipping again (this could take 30 seconds to a minute). Dip quickly so the wax that is already on the wick doesn't melt off. Let it cool completely each time.

As the wax starts to build up around the wick, it will begin to look like a candle. You can add some more wax to the can if you need to. Continue dipping until the candle is about three-quarters of an inch in diameter at the bottom. Once the wax is fully dried, cut the candle free from the wooden spoon, leaving about a half-inch of wick.

trim -------

When you get good at this, experiment with color by having several coffee cans of different-colored wax heating on the stove. Can you figure out how to dip the candles to get stripes?

Make Your Own

SPATTERWARE
CROCK

SUPPLIES

- newspaper
- wax paper
- masking tape
- 2 pounds of self-hardening clay
- an old dinner knife
- craft stick
- thick paintbrush
- thin paintbrush
- blue and white acrylic paint
- small dish

Spatterware is brightly colored pottery. It was made in England and sold in the United States in the mid-1800s. The designs are either "spattered" on or put on with a sponge. This is the kind of pottery pioneers had with them as they traveled west, or what they might have found at a trading post because it was cheap and durable.

1 Spread the newspaper over your work area, and then tape a length of waxed paper over the newspaper. This is where you'll do your clay work.

2 Work the clay with your hands to soften it, making it easier to shape. Carefully use the knife to cut off a chunk of clay for the base of your crock. Shape it into a circle about 5 inches in diameter and about a half-inch thick. Use the craft stick to smooth off the top of the base.

3 Take another chunk of clay and roll it out into a long rope about a half-inch thick. Fit this around the top of the base and pinch the ends together. Make more ropes of clay and place each one on top of the previous one. As you build the walls, smooth the inside and outside of the pot to make the seams invisible. You can use the craft stick for this. Remember

that you can taper the sides in or leave them straight. Just make sure the sides are thick enough so they won't collapse. When your pot is about 6 inches high, put it aside to harden.

4 After your pot has hardened paint it blue. When this has dried, pour some of the white paint into a small dish and dip your small paintbrush into it. Now flick your paintbrush toward your pot. DO THIS OUTSIDE OR IN AN AREA WHERE IT IS OKAY TO MAKE A MESS. This will create the spatter effect. Let your paint dry.

FUN AND HOLIDAYS

LIFE AS A PIONEER WAS HARD WORK, so it was important for families to figure out how to entertain themselves. During work bees, the men socialized while building barns or houses together, and during quilting bees the women socialized. Sometimes everyone who lived in the area would gather in someone's barn for a barn dance. The fiddle was a pretty common instrument in those days and in any group you could find someone who knew how to play. But these social gatherings were a rare treat. Most of the time families had to entertain themselves by making candy, inventing and playing games, reading aloud to each other, or by telling stories.

There wasn't much play time on the frontier because there was always something that had to be done: fences needed to be built, clothes needed to be washed and mended, cows needed to be milked, eggs needed to be gathered. Frontier families really looked forward to holidays because it meant a change from the hard routine of daily life and it was a chance to gather and relax with the neighbors. The biggest holidays on the frontier were Independence Day, Thanksgiving, and Christmas.

Independence Day

In the 1930s the federal government paid writers to go around the country and conduct oral history interviews with people. These oral history projects provide a real insight into how people lived in the last part of the nineteenth century and the first part of the twentieth century.

Here's what Miss Nettie Spencer from Portland, Oregon, said about the Fourth of July on the frontier in the 1870s.

"There would be floats in the morning and the one that got the eye was the Goddess of Liberty. She was supposed to be the most wholesome and prettiest girl in the countryside. Following the float would be the Oregon Agricultural College cadets, and some kind of a band. Sometimes there would be political effigies.

Just before lunch—and we'd always hold lunch up for an hour—some Senator or lawyer would speak. These speeches always had one pattern. First the speaker would challenge England to a fight and berate the King and say that he was a skunk. This was known as twisting the lion's tail. Then the next theme was that any one could find freedom and liberty on our shores. The speaker would invite those who were heavy laden in other lands to come to us and find peace. The speeches were pretty fiery and the men called each other Englishmen. In the afternoon we had what we called the 'plug uglies' — funny floats and clowns who took off on the political subjects of the day . . . The Fourth was the day of the year that really counted then. Christmas wasn't much; a Church tree or something, but no one twisted the lion's tail."

"Rural Life in the 1870s,"
Portland, Oregon,
Walker Winslow, interviewer, December 15, 1938.
American Life Histories, 1936–1940

Thanksgiving Day was celebrated at the table, much the way it is today. The family would feast on roast wild turkey or goose, potatoes, corn, wild nuts they had gathered, and pies. It was a day to gather with family and friends and enjoy each other's company. Unlike today, there were no afternoon football games on television!

Like Thanksgiving, Christmas was a time to celebrate the company of loved ones. If possible, pioneer families would decorate their log cabins or soddies with pine boughs, pine cones, and a tree that they had cut down from the woods. Pioneers would deck their tree with ribbon, paper cut-outs, and salt dough ornaments. Children would also string popcorn and berries on thread and wrap them around the tree. Instead of strands of Christmas lights, they placed small candles on the boughs of the tree, which they'd light and monitor very carefully to prevent fires. There was always a bucket of water nearby!

A wild turkey.

Christmas gifts were small and handmade. Children might receive a new knit hat or scarf or a pair of mittens from their mother. Father might have had time to carve a toy or doll for the youngest children. A trip to the mercantile or general store around Christmas time might mean there'd be some penny candy or marbles in the stockings.

Make Your Own
OLD-FASHIONED MOLASSES TAFFY

Many pioneers preferred the taste of molasses to white table sugar, because it's what they were used to Back East. Every trading post and mercantile had barrels of molasses. The molasses-hungry pioneer would bring a container to fill.

1 Combine the butter, sugar, molasses, water, and corn syrup in the large pot. Place the pot over high heat and stir constantly until the sugar dissolves. Cook rapidly, lowering the heat slightly as the mixture thickens. Keep cooking until the temperature on your candy thermometer reads 258 degrees Fahrenheit. This is called the "hard ball" stage in candy.

2 Pour the candy into the pan and allow it to cool just enough so that you can handle it. Butter your hands lightly and make the taffy into a ball, then begin to pull the candy until it is light in color and becomes too hard to pull. Stretch the taffy into a long rope about a half-inch in diameter and then cut it into 1-inch pieces with scissors. This step can be really messy!

3 Wrap the pieces of candy in waxed paper, twisting both ends. This recipe makes about 1½ pounds of individual taffy candies.

SUPPLIES

* ½ cup melted butter
* 2 cups sugar
* 1 cup molasses
* 1½ cups water
* ¼ cup light corn syrup
* large pot
* wooden spoon
* candy thermometer
* large shallow pan greased with butter
* extra butter
* scissors
* squares of waxed paper

Make Your Own
BALL AND CUP GAME

A fun pioneer game involves trying to catch a ball with a cup. Children on the frontier had a lot of daily chores to do but they also had time for some fun. This was a simple toy that took some skill to get good at, so when kids who played this game had a little spare time they would practice. Then, when these kids met up with friends they would have competitions. You'll see for yourself that it's harder than it looks!

1 Cut an 18-inch length of string. Stick the straight pin in the ball and, before pushing it all the way in, tie or wrap one end of the string around it. Then shove the pin all the way into the ball.

2 Hold the cup with the open end facing up, then punch a hole up through the center of the bottom of the paper cup with a pencil. Push the dowel up about an inch through this hole, and then tie the free end of the string to the very bottom part of the dowel (the part that is not poking through the bottom of the cup). Tape the string to the dowel to make it secure.

3 Take some clay and pack it around the dowel inside the cup. Build it up so that it covers the top of the dowel. Let the clay dry.

4 Your game is ready. To play, hold the dowel and try to swing the ball up into the cup. Have tournaments with your friends to see how many times in a row you can catch the ball in the cup.

SUPPLIES

* string
* measuring tape
* scissors
* straight pin
* 2-inch Styrofoam ball
* paper cup
* pencil
* thin, 12-inch dowel
* tape
* air-hardening clay

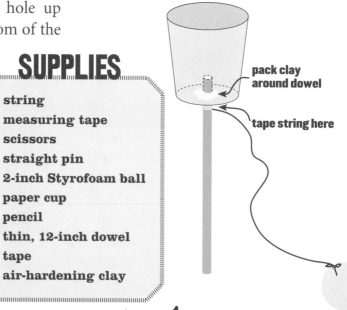

pack clay around dowel

tape string here

Make Your Own
DRIED APPLE DOLL

Pioneers had to use whatever they had on hand when they made toys. Dried apple dolls were popular in the nineteenth century because most people had access to apples.

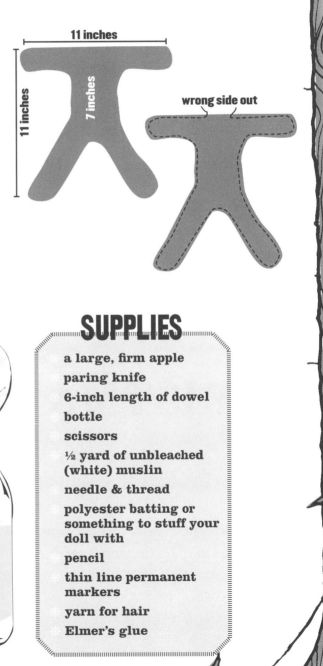

1 Peel the skin off your apple with the paring knife. Carve the face on one side with an exaggerated nose and chin.

2 Force the dowel about an inch into the apple where the neck would be. Put the dowel in the bottle so the apple head stands up and put it in a cool, dry place to dry out. Be sure to check it every few days because if it starts to get moldy you'll have to throw it away and start again. Over several days the apple head will dry out and get very withered.

3 While the head is drying, make the doll body. Using the pattern at right, cut two pieces out of the muslin. Placing the right sides together, sew all the way around the doll body, leaving the shoulders and neck open.

carve the face and stand in a bottle to dry

11 inches

11 inches

7 inches

wrong side out

SUPPLIES

* a large, firm apple
* paring knife
* 6-inch length of dowel
* bottle
* scissors
* ½ yard of unbleached (white) muslin
* needle & thread
* polyester batting or something to stuff your doll with
* pencil
* thin line permanent markers
* yarn for hair
* Elmer's glue

97

4 Turn the doll body right side out and stuff the body with the batting—use a pencil to help get the batting into the arms and legs. Make sure you put as much batting in as you can to make the doll body firm.

5 Once your apple head is dried, use fine markers to draw in the eyes and mouth. Maybe put a bit of red on the cheeks. Cut 3- or 4-inch-long pieces of yarn and glue these onto the apple head for hair. You can make a little hat with leftover muslin to cover where you've glued on the hair.

6 Place the doll head onto the body by forcing the dowel down into the batting. Pack more batting around the dowel at the neck to make it as stiff as possible. Sew the shoulders and neck shut using thread that matches the muslin and little stitches.

stitch remaing opening

draw face on the doll and glue on hair

Make Your Own
SALT DOUGH
CHRISTMAS ORNAMENTS

1 Turn on the oven to 300 degrees Fahrenheit. Grease the cookie sheets with the oil and paper towel.

2 Combine 2 cups of the flour and the salt in the mixing bowl. Slowly stir in the water a little at a time. When the dough becomes thick, use your hands to mix it well.

3 Spread some flour on a pastry board or table and put the dough on the flour and knead. Make sure your hands have flour on them and place the heels of your palms into the dough and then fold it over. The more you knead the dough, the more it changes in consistency. Knead for about 5 or 10 minutes until it feels a bit harder and smooth, like clay. You can add a little more flour as needed.

4 Roll the dough out on the floured surface with the rolling pin until it's no more than a half-inch thick. Cut shapes out of the dough with the cookie cutters. Use leftover dough for adding details like eyes and mouths, or berries, etc. Use the knitting needle to make a hole at the top of each ornament so you can thread them with string when you're finished. Place the ornaments on the cookie sheets. making sure they are not touching.

5 Bake your ornaments for about an hour. They should be very hard when finished. After the ornaments are thoroughly cool you can decorate them with paints. If you cover the ornaments entirely with paint it will seal them from moisture, meaning they could last for several years.

6 Finish your ornaments by stringing six inches of yarn or string through each ornament. They are ready to hang up for the holidays! Store your ornaments wrapped up in waxed paper or in sandwich bags. Put them in a container with a lid, like a shoebox.

SUPPLIES

- **2 cookie sheets**
- **1 tablespoon cooking oil**
- **paper towels**
- **2 cups flour plus extra**
- **1 cup salt**
- **1½ cups water**
- **large mixing bowl**
- **wooden spoon**
- **rolling pin**
- **ruler**
- **cookie cutters**
- **knitting needle**
- **cookie sheets**
- **acrylic paints**
- **colored yarn or string**

COWBOYS AND INDIANS

AS THE COUNTRY EXPANDED FROM THE 1860S THROUGH the mid-1880s, the demand for beef in both the new territories and established states grew quickly. The railroad moved cattle from Texas and the Southwest to areas where beef was in demand. But someone had to get the cattle to the railroads, and that's where **cowboys** came in. Cowboys were men who rounded up herds of cattle and drove them north to the railroad. This isn't the kind of driving you know about! When cowboys drove cattle north they rounded them up into a group by riding around them, then got them moving in a certain direction. Over several weeks the cattle would walk all the way to the railroad, with cowboys on horseback keeping them moving along. From there, cattle were loaded into cattle cars and shipped to **slaughterhouses** all over the country.

Most cowboys signed on for a season, which was an individual **round up** and **cattle drive**. For most of the year, cattle were left to graze in the prairie. Then twice a year cowboys rounded them up, gathering and sorting them according to the ranch that owned them. It was easy to tell which cattle belonged to which ranch, because the calves were all **branded**. Cowboys separated the male cattle, called steers, that were ready for market out into a herd.

Cowboys worked in groups, called "outfits." Outfits had a trail boss, a straw boss, a cook, and a **remuda** man. The trail boss was the leader. The straw boss was second in command. The cook was responsible for the food and the **chuck wagon**. Food, medicines, and firewood went in the chuck wagon. And the remuda man was in charge of the extra horses.

There was usually about one cowboy for every 300 head of cattle, and each cowboy had between five and nine extra horses in the remuda. So there was always a fresh horse to ride when a cowboy's horse got tired or injured.

Word Round-Up

cowboy: Someone on horseback who tended and drove herds of cattle, particularly in western United States and Canada.

slaughterhouse: The place where animals are butchered for market.

round up: Cowboys gathered the cattle in one place twice a year to brand the calves and separate out cattle for market.

cattle drive: Moving a herd of cattle from one place to another—cowboys would get them going and then keep them moving in the right direction.

brand: To permanently mark a cow or horse with the symbol of a ranch.

remuda: From the Spanish word for exchange, this was the herd of extra horses for the cowboys.

chuck wagon: A wagon with a stove and provisions for cooking, as well as medicines and firewood.

Branding cattle.

Each cowboy had an assigned place during the drive. Point men rode up front on either side of the herd and flank riders rode beside the herd. The men who "rode drag" looking for stragglers and lost cattle were at the back of the herd. The youngest and least experienced cowboys were the ones who usually ended up riding drag because it was the dustiest place to be.

The biggest challenges facing the cowboys were cattle thieves, storms, prairie fires, unfriendly Native Americans, and **stampedes**. Since cattle are group animals, if one starts to run the others follow. The longhorn stampedes were the worst, because longhorns are the most fierce and powerful of all cattle. As the cattle headed north from Texas and crossed the Red River, they entered **Indian Territory**, an area of land that had been given to many Native American tribes by the government. There, the cowboys had to pay a **toll** to the Native Americans, ranging from ten cents to a dollar per head of cattle.

DID YOU KNOW?

Cattle are counted by the head, so if a ranch owned 300 cows you would say they had 300 head of cattle. Cowboys are counted as hands, so they might have said, "how many hands will go on the cattle drive?"

A steer worth $4 in Texas might be worth $40 farther north. The more north the cowboys could get the beef, the higher the price they could get for it. When it came to beef, there was never a shortage of want or need. The government needed it to feed troops stationed throughout the West and the Native Americans on reservations they had promised to feed. Homesteaders and people in towns along the railroads wanted beef. And easterners wanted beef, too. Every longhorn brought to the slaughterhouses eventually ended up on someone's plate.

By the mid-1880s, all the Texas Longhorns had been driven up the trail from Texas. About 5 million of them made it to Kansas. Some went farther north

Texas Longhorns

These wiry cattle with long horns are descendents from cattle brought to the Americas by the Spanish in the sixteenth century. Mexicans raised these cattle for many years, but some got loose and headed north. Eventually a herd developed in Texas that was a cross between the wiry Mexican cattle and the Anglo cattle. The new breed was strong, intelligent, and deadly when provoked. In 1865 it was estimated that there were about 5 million longhorns roaming western Texas.

but almost a million died on the trail. About 1,000 cowboys also died on the trail, mainly by stampedes. Being a cowboy was tough, dangerous work, and the pay was low (between $50 and $90 per cattle drive, which took a few months). For that reason, many cowboys retired from the trail at a young age.

Cowboy Clothing

Cowboys wore long trousers and long-sleeved shirts. They tucked their trousers into knee-high boots. The boots had pointy toes to slip into their stirrups quickly, high heels to keep their feet in the stirrups, and decorative stitching to keep the leather boot stiff. The high boot protected legs from thorns, brush, and snakes. **Chaps** were often strapped around the legs to give them further protection. Many cowboys sewed a piece of leather onto the seat of their trousers that extended down the inside of their legs so that their pants wouldn't wear out so quickly from sitting on the horse so much.

Cowboy hats were different, depending on where in the country they were made. Southwest hats were tall with a wide brim to offer maximum protection from the hot desert sun. Hats from the Northern Plains were not as tall, had a narrow brim, and sat lower on the head so they wouldn't blow away.

Word
Round-Up

stampede: A sudden uncontrolled rush of a group of animals.

Indian Territory: An area designated by Congress in the 1830s. It stretched from Texas to the Missouri River in what is present-day Oklahoma. Native Americans from the East were forced from their homelands and sent to live in the Indian Territory. Later, most of this land became open to white homesteaders during the Oklahoma Land Rush of 1889.

toll: A tax or fee paid for the right to pass through an area or over a road or bridge.

chaps: Seatless leggings worn by cowboys for protection of their legs while on horseback.

Spurs were metal wheels with sharp points. Cowboys attached spurs to their boot heels and used them for urging a horse forward. As cowboys walked across wooden boardwalks in towns, spurs made a jingle-jangle sound.

Bandanas were another must-have for the cowboys. Bandanas were usually red or blue—they could not be white because white reflected light and scared cattle. Normally, cowboys folded their bandana into a triangle and tied it around their neck. If a cowboy was riding drag he could pull it up over his nose and mouth to avoid breathing in the clouds of dust. If it was very sunny, windy, or snowy, he could tie it around his neck to prevent sunburn or cold. At the end of the day, cowboys could wet their bandana and use it to wash their faces. Cowboys also used bandanas to cover the eyes of a nervous horse, and to signal to other cowboys.

A cowboy couldn't keep anything in his pants pockets when he was sitting on his horse, so he used his large vest pockets. Typically, a cowboy also wore a long canvas coat and kept a rain slicker tied with his bedroll behind his saddle.

Popular Cowboy Trails

In 1866 Charles Goodnight and Oliver Loving drove a herd of 2,000 longhorns from west Texas to New Mexico. Called the Goodnight-Loving Trail, it extended up into Colorado and Wyoming, and ended in Miles City, Montana. The Western Trail began in San Antonio, Texas, and headed north through Indian Territory, Dodge City, Ogallala Territory (Nebraska), and up into the Dakota Territory. The Chisholm Trail also began in San Antonio and went through Indian Territory up into Wichita and Abilene. The Shawnee Trail began in southern Texas and headed north and east through Dallas and straight into Kansas City (with an off-shoot going to St. Louis).

Native Americans in the West

As pioneers moved westward they met Native Americans who had been living in the West long before the Europeans arrived in the Americas. The first Native Americans came to North America at least 12,000 years ago. By the time the pioneers began pushing west, there were about 200 different native tribes living west of the Missouri River. Some of these tribes had been forced west by Europeans settling in the East. These Native Americans had unique cultures and languages that had been established and evolved over the course of hundreds or even thousands of years. Although the United States made treaties with many of these tribes, over the years these treaties were broken by the government. As more Americans sought land or gold on native lands—as was the case in the **Black Hills**—the U.S. government always sided with its own people.

From 1860 through the 1880s, the story of what happened to the western Native Americans is marked by broken promises and broken treaties, the widespread killing of buffalo, and frequent battles between various tribes and the U.S. government. These battles were called the **Indian Wars**. During the years of the Indian Wars, the U.S. government built military forts throughout the West—both to protect the settlers from Native Americans and to relocate the Native people to reservations. There were dozens of battles between soldiers and the tribes of the Plains and Southwest. The massacre at Wounded Knee, South Dakota, in 1890 is generally considered the end of the Indian Wars. The violence of this event began while U.S. troops were gathering Lakota Sioux Indians with orders to transport them by rail to Omaha, Nebraska. Suddenly a gunshot went off. To this day, accounts differ as to who fired that first shot and

why, but immediately afterwards there was chaotic gunfire coming from both sides. When the shooting was over 153 Sioux and 25 soldiers had been killed.

✆ Overheard: Sweet Medicine ✆

"There are all kinds of people on earth that you will meet someday. There will be many of these people, so many that you cannot stand against them . . . They will try to change you from your way of living to theirs, and they will keep at what they try to do."

Cheyenne prophet

The All-Important Buffalo

The Plains Indians relied on the buffalo for everything—food, clothing, shelter, and even medicine. As pioneers moved west into Indian Territory, followed by professional buffalo hunters and the railroad, the buffalo population dropped quickly. This was one of the worst effects that the pioneers had on Plains Indians, and one of the biggest reasons why violence broke out between the native people and white settlers.

Native Americans used buffalo hides to make cradles for babies, and for curtains, tepee walls, clothing, and blankets. Sometimes the hides were stretched out until they were very tight and used as a canvas to paint images. Native Americans used buffalo tails as flyswatters, wove the hair into rope, or used it for stuffing pillows, moccasins, and gloves. And it didn't stop there! Buffalo horns and bones were made into spoons, cups, knives, and tools, and buffalo ribs were used for frames in small sleds.

Before the railroads were built, it had been almost impossible to get buffalo meat and untanned buffalo hides to market in the East before they spoiled. Trains made it all possible. People Back East wanted more and more buffalo. Buffalo meat was lean and tasty and the hides made terrific clothing and material. The bones made excellent fertilizer.

With the railroads in place, professional buffalo hunters took an estimated 4,374,000 buffalo from the Southern Plains in the early 1870s. Native Americans, who relied on the buffalo for everything, killed about a quarter of that number during this same time period. At the beginning of the nineteenth century there were about 30 million buffalo roaming the Great Plains. By 1883, a team of scientists sent from Washington to count the buffalo found only 200 left on the prairie!

Word *Round-Up*

Black Hills: The sacred lands of the Lakota people in what is now South Dakota. When gold was discovered there prospectors overran the area. This led to a conflict between the Lakota and the U.S. Army.

Indian Wars: A series of conflicts between the United States and Native Americans.

As the buffalo disappeared, the Plains Indians found themselves facing starvation in a land that had once held plentiful resources. This made it easier for the U.S. government to force the Native Americans onto reservations. With no food to eat, Native Americans had few choices. They had to believe in the promise of food and a better life from the U.S. government.

The government policy was to try to "Americanize" the Native Americans by making them into farmers and homesteaders on reservations. They set up boarding schools for Native American children and often sent them far away from their families. These children had their hair cut and they were dressed in "American" clothes. They were even punished if they spoke their native language.

Ghost Dance

The Ghost Dance movement swept through the Sioux nation in 1890. The Sioux believed that if they participated in a Ghost Dance Ceremony, their ancestors would come back, as would the buffalo. The movement became popular because the Sioux saw it as a way of bringing back the old times—before the white settlers had taken over their land and forced them to change their lifestyle. At the ceremony, participants danced in a circle while tribal and community leaders went into a trance and prophesized. The ceremony lasted 5 days. The Sioux also believe if you wore something called a Ghost Dance shirt, soldiers' bullets couldn't harm you. The Ghost Dance movement made the U.S. Army nervous because they didn't understand it and believed it made the Native Americans more defiant.

Make Your Own MINIATURE TEPEE

Because the Plains Indians followed the buffalo, they carried their homes—tepees—with them. The tepee cover was made from buffalo hides sewn together. It weighed about 150 pounds! Native American women could set up or take down a tepee in just minutes.

1 Bunch your twigs or dowels together. Wrap the cord around them four or five times about 1½ inches from one end. Tie it off. Now spread open the long ends of the dowels and you will have the frame of the tepee.

2 Cut the felt using the dimensions and following the pattern provided. Use indelible markers to decorate your teepee. The Plains Indians would often make their teepee covers very colorful.

3 Make a mark every three-quarter inch along both edges of the opening of the tepee. This is where you're going to close the tepee using your leather laces. Using your scissors, make holes where you've marked the felt.

4 Place the felt around the frame putting the top edge below where the cord wrapping begins. Now "lace" your tepee shut by running the leather lace through the holes beginning at the top.

lacing the teepee

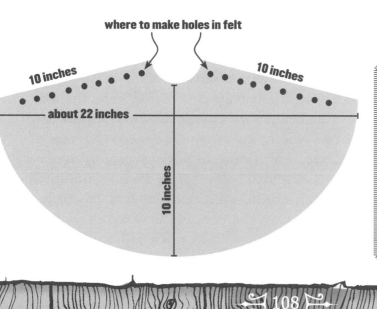

where to make holes in felt

10 inches   10 inches

about 22 inches

10 inches

SUPPLIES

* 6 straight twigs, each at least 1 foot long, or 6 thin dowels
* hemp or cotton cord
* 2 feet of tan felt or chamois cloth
* scissors
* indelible markers
* ruler
* leather lacing or 2 leather shoe laces

DOCUMENTING THE WEST

BY THE SECOND HALF OF THE NINETEENTH CENTURY, photography was quite common. While cameras and photographs had been around since 1837, photography really took off after the Civil War. Famous photographers like Mathew Brady took more than 5,000 images of the Civil War between 1860 and 1865. This helped make cameras and photographs popular. By the 1880s photographers traveled through the Plains and took portraits of pioneer families along the way.

A photographer's wagon.

Mathew Brady—Civil War Photographer

Mathew Brady was the most famous photographer in the United States in the nineteenth century. He learned photography when it was still in its earliest stages, and he set up a studio in New York where he concentrated on **portraiture**. Later he moved his studio to Washington, DC, and became interested in recording historic events. Beginning in 1861 he headed a group of photographers who photographed many of the major battles of the Civil War. His photographs of the dead and dying soldiers shocked the American public. *The New York Times* wrote that Brady had brought "home to us the terrible reality and earnestness of war." After the Civil War when people were tired of seeing his graphic images, Brady went bankrupt. He had sunk all of his money into creating his Civil War pictures. Eventually, Congress realized the

Mathew Brady

importance of Brady's work and purchased his archives, but not before he died penniless. To honor Brady's work, he was buried in Arlington National Cemetery.

Wild Bill Hickock (top) and Buffalo Bill Cody (bottom)

There are no photographs of the earliest pioneers traveling west in the 1840s. A few photographers, however, made the journey in the middle of the century, photographing the beauty of the vast American landscape. Painters and photographers traveled with government-sponsored scientific expeditions. William Henry Jackson and Timothy O'Sullivan were two of the photographers whose job it was to document the West. They carried bulky photographic equipment wherever they went. The scenes they brought back captured the imagination of many easterners and inspired them to pack up their belongings and head Out West for a new adventure.

William Henry Jackson (1843–1942) and Timothy H. O'Sullivan (1840–1882)

William Henry Jackson is best known for his photos of the land that would become our first national park, Yellowstone. Jackson went all over the West, from the **badlands** of Wyoming to the cliff dwellings of Arizona and New Mexico. Timothy O'Sullivan's photographs show the beautiful way rock formations look in the light of the barren lands of the Southwest.

Photograph of an alpine lake in the Sierra Nevada in California, taken by O'Sullivan in 1871.

Later in the 1800s, photographers became more commonplace. They took photographs of people who were well-known western figures, like Wild Bill Hickock and Buffalo Bill Cody, and of somber-faced families who lived and worked out on the prairie.

Native American Portraits

In 1832, George Catlin (1796–1872) headed up the Missouri River to the Fort Union trading post in the Dakota Territory. He was determined to see and paint the native people in their "unspoiled" state. Over the course of two trips Catlin painted 500 images called *Catlin's Indian Gallery*.

Photograph of the view down a canyon to a river. Taken in Colorado by Jackson.

Another book that featured images of Native Americans was called *A History of the Indian Tribes of North America*. The Office of Indian Affairs distributed this book. Each volume contained nearly 150 portraits, mainly by Charles Bird King (1785–1862), and these became the best known portraits of Native Americans before the Civil War.

The Catlin and Bird paintings were not accurate. They were idealized images of Native Americans (mainly Plains

Choo Ca Pe, chief of the Otoe tribe painted by Charles Bird King.

Word Round-Up

portraiture: The art of drawing or taking a picture of someone.

badlands: A dry region characterized by steeply eroded rock and fantastically formed hills.

dime novel: Swift-moving, thrilling novels, mainly about the American Revolution, the frontier period, and the Civil War. The books were first sold in 1860 for ten cents.

Wild West shows: A spectacular show organized in 1883 by William F. Cody, nicknamed Buffalo Bill. The show featured horseback riding and marksmanship demonstrations and exhibited the wild spirit of the West.

Annie Oakley: An excellent marksman in Buffalo Bill's Wild West show. She would break small glass balls by looking at a mirror and shooting her rifle backward over her shoulder.

silhouette: An outline of somebody or something filled in with blackness or shadow.

Indians) in the early part of the nineteenth century. This means the paintings showed the Native Americans as the artists wanted them to be, showing their lives more pleasant or better than they were. These were the first images many pioneers saw of the Native Americans they might encounter on the trail.

Read all about it!

As groupings of houses became organized settlements, people began publishing newspapers. Just like newspaper companies today, frontier newspaper businesses made money by selling advertisements and subscriptions. Wherever there were businesses, there was potential income for the newspaper. Everyone hungered for the news—any news—because it was a source of entertainment that broke up the often lonely and hard, work-filled days.

One column that was in every early paper was the local "comin's and goin's" column—a list of who was seen visiting whom. They also carried national and state news, letters, editorials, and lots of ads.

After the railroads and the telegraph came through a town, newspaper editors would get state and national news from the big city newspapers or over the telegraph wire. Newspapers were also seen as an effective way to get people to move to a certain area. Editors who were good at promoting a region were called "booming" editors.

Laying out a newspaper in those days was not an easy task. The movable type (movable because each letter was separate) was placed on racks to make words. This took a lot of thinking and planning. The letters were backwards so that when they printed the words would be correct, so being able to read letters backwards was a big help, too.

The Sensational West

Aside from occasional letters and newspapers, how did people Back East learn about the West? The **dime novel** and **Wild West shows**. Dime novels first showed up in the 1860s and cost—you guessed it—a dime.

A dime novel from Beadle & Company.

These paperbacks sold amazingly well and in the first 4 years of business the main publisher of these novels, the House of Beadle and Adams, sold 5 million copies. Dime novels were often serialized in newspapers. This means they were published in pieces, one at a time over several weeks or months. The dime novel western always placed a lone, tough hero in the wide open spaces of the western frontier. The hero could fight Indians (and win) and endure the elements in this landscape. This became the common view of the West.

In the 1870s dime novelist Ned Buntline began writing about William F. Cody, whom he called, "Buffalo Bill, the King of the Border Men." William F. Cody, the wildly popular hero of the dime novels, was a well-known scout for the frontier army. In close to 150 dime novels, Buffalo Bill came to represent the West.

In 1883, William F. Cody opened his "Wild West, Rocky Mountain, and Prairie Exhibition." Later the name changed to "Buffalo Bill's Wild West and Congress of Rough Riders of the World." People flocked to Cody's shows, convinced he was showing them the real Wild West. It was part circus, and part pageant. He recreated so-called historical reenactments of events, like the defeat of General George A. Custer at Little Bighorn, and featured rodeo tricks like bulldogging and rope twirling. **Annie Oakley** was just one of the superior marksmen who dazzled audiences with her shooting prowess. But what most fascinated audiences were the Native Americans wearing beautiful headdresses who rode into the arena on horses. In 1885, Chief Sitting Bull, the most famous Native American of the time, joined the Wild West show for one year.

A poster advertising Buffalo Bill's Wild West show.

Make Your Own
PINHOLE CAMERA

An ordinary camera has a lens that captures an image on film. In a pinhole camera your lens is actually a small hole. For thousands of years people have recognized that you could capture a panoramic view through a pin-sized hole, but in 1837 Louis Daguerre figured out how to capture an image on a light-sensitive surface.

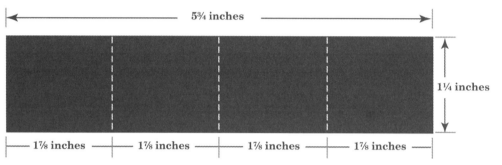

5¾ inches

1¼ inches

1⅞ inches | 1⅞ inches | 1⅞ inches | 1⅞ inches

1 Measure and cut out a rectangle from the cardboard that is 5¾ inches long by 1¼ inches wide. Paint one side of the cardboard with flat black paint (not glossy) or cover it with black paper. Measure and mark every 1⅞ inches along the top and bottom of the long side of your rectangle. Run your sharp knife along the cardboard in straight lines from the top to bottom marks. Don't cut through the cardboard, just score it enough to make it easier to fold. Fold the cardboard into a box and tape it with black tape. The box should have two open ends.

SUPPLIES

* corrugated cardboard from a box or the cardboard back of a pad of paper
* scissors
* ruler
* pencil
* flat black paint & brush
* black paper
* sharp knife
* black tape
* one cartridge of 110 size color film (ASA 200 works best)
* aluminum foil
* sewing needle
* 2 large rubber bands
* 1 nickel—use a new Buffalo nickel in honor of the American West

2 Put one open end of the box into the film cartridge between the two "humps." It should be a snug fit.

3 To make the front of the camera, cut another piece of cardboard that measures 2¾ inches by 1½ inches. Paint one side with the flat black paint or cover it with black paper. Measure and cut a half-inch-square hole in the center of this cardboard and carefully tape a 1-inch square of aluminum foil over the unpainted side of

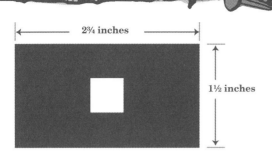

2¾ inches

1½ inches

the hole. Now make a tiny pin prick with your needle right in the center of the foil. Keep the hole as small as possible.

4 Use your two rubber bands to attach the "front" of the camera to the camera body. Make sure that no light is getting into the inside of the camera, because if it does, the picture will not be as sharp. Cover any holes or openings with black tape.

5 Cut a 1-inch square of black paper and tape it to the top of the aluminum foil. This needs to cover the pinhole when the camera is not in use.

6 Insert your buffalo nickel into the slot on top of the film and advance the film by turning counterclockwise, to the left. The small window on the side of the film will tell you what number frame you're on. Note that each number shows up several times so always keep going past the first time you see the number.

7 To take a photograph with your new camera, you must keep it as still as possible. Find a way to place the camera on a solid surface that's not going to move while you're exposing the film. There's no viewfinder to look through to see exactly what the camera sees so you have guess where to place it.

8 When you're ready to take the photo, open up the black flap in front of the pinhole and expose the film for several seconds. You're going to have to experiment with exposure time and it would be a good idea to keep a little notebook recording how long each frame was exposed. Take the same image a few times varying the exposure time to see what works best. You might also want to vary the position of the camera to make sure you get it right.

9 Take a portrait of your family, just like some of the posed portraits you've seen in this book, to create a family heirloom. When you get your film processed, you'll be amazed at your new-found artistic abilities.

Make Your Own

SILHOUETTE

Many people could not afford a photographic portrait and photographers didn't make it to every remote homestead. Pioneer families could still make lasting portraits with a **silhouette**. This is an outline of somebody or something filled in with blackness or shadow. Sometimes you can find these framed silhouettes in antique stores today. Miniature silhouettes were also created and placed in lockets.

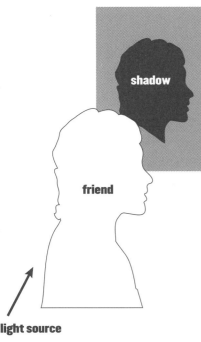

friend

shadow

light source

1 Place your straight-backed chair with its side nearly touching the wall and have your friend sit in it. Position the light so that it shines directly onto the side of your friend's face, casting a shadow on the wall.

2 Tape a sheet of white paper onto the wall where the shadow falls. If the outline is blurry, have your friend move closer to the wall until it is clear. Trace the outline of the shadow onto the white paper.

3 Take the paper off the wall and carefully cut out the profile. Place the cut-out profile on to the black construction paper and trace around it with your pencil. Carefully cut the silhouette out of the black paper.

4 Center the silhouette onto a plain sheet of white paper and glue it down. Put your name and date in a corner.

5 Now you sit in the chair and have your friend trace your silhouette. Repeat steps three and four. Wouldn't this make a nice gift for your parents?

SUPPLIES

* straight-backed chair
* friend
* blank wall
* bright light like a flashlight or desk lamp
* a few sheets of plain white paper
* tape
* pencil
* scissors
* black construction paper
* glue

Make Your Own NEWSPAPER

Print your own newspaper using movable type made out of pasta letters!

1 Plan out what you want your newspaper to look like and what kind of news you want to cover. It could be family events or national news. Look at the size of your letters. This will determine how much text can go on a page. Write out some brief stories and headlines. If you want your text to be in columns then write it out that way. Study a real newspaper to see what this looks like.

2 Draw lines on the cardboard with your ruler so you can line up your letters. Pour your alphabet letters onto a plate.

3 Line the letters up above the first line you're going to make. Everything needs to be backwards, INCLUDING YOUR LETTERS. One way to make sure you're laying them out correctly is to hold a mirror up to the words you've formed and see if you can read them. If you can, you're on the right track.

4 After you've laid out the letters correctly, put some glue on the line you're working on and move your letters down to the line. Repeat this for every line you're going to print, and for each page.

5 Squirt some ink into the disposable bowl. Dip your sponge into the ink (don't put too much ink on the sponge) and then blot it onto the letters. It doesn't matter if it goes down between the letters but don't gunk it up too much.

6 Place your inked cardboard face down on a sheet of paper and carefully place the book on top of the cardboard. If you move the paper or the cardboard it will smudge. Let it sit for a minute or two and then very carefully remove the book and lift the cardboard off your paper. Repeat this process for each page of your newspaper.

7 You can make several copies of your newspaper. Re-ink your letters in between sheets when necessary.

SUPPLIES

- scrap paper
- pencil
- heavy pieces of cardboard slightly smaller than your sheets of paper
- ruler
- plate
- uncooked alphabet pasta
- tweezers
- hand mirror
- glue
- water soluble block print ink from a craft store
- small disposable bowl
- sponge
- sheets of white paper
- large, heavy book

MOM GETS
AWARD

LET'S CONGRATULATE
MOM ON THE AWARD
SHE GOT.

GLOSSARY

100th meridian: The longitude line running down through the center of the country.

A

adobe: Building material of sun-dried earth and straw.

annex: To take possession or control of something.

Annie Oakley: An excellent marksman in Buffalo Bill's Wild West show. She would break small glass balls by looking at a mirror and shooting her rifle backward over her shoulder.

archaeologist: Someone who studies past human life and culture by finding and examining things like graves, ruins, tools, and pottery.

B

badlands: A dry region characterized by steeply eroded rock and fantastically formed hills.

bee: A social gathering where people in a community helped a family clear land for farming, or raise a barn. Every member of the community eventually benefited from a bee.

Black Hills: The sacred lands of the Lakota people in what is now South Dakota. When gold was discovered there prospectors overran the area. This led to a conflict between the Lakota and the U.S. Army.

booming editors: Editors who were good at promoting the frontier region where they lived.

brand: To permanently mark a cow or horse with the symbol of a ranch.

broadside: Poster advertisements of the West.

Buffalo Bill: A legendary buffalo hunter who capitalized on his fame by developing a "Wild West" show that presented the history of the West in a colorful and romanticized way.

buffalo chips: Dried buffalo dung that was used for fuel. It burned hot and clean.

C

California Trail: An off-shoot of the Oregon Trail that led emigrants southwest to California.

Californios: Spanish-speaking California natives who settled in the area many years before the American emigrants.

Carson, Kit: A mountain man and explorer who is best known for leading the Apaches and the Navajos on the "Long Walk," a forced march of 300 miles during which hundreds of Navajo died.

cartographer: A person who makes maps.

cattle drive: Moving a herd of cattle from one place to another—cowboys would get them going and then keep them moving in the right direction.

chaps: Seatless leggings worn by cowboys for protection of their legs while on horseback.

Chimney Rock: A large pyramid-shaped reddish rock with a 100-foot spire, the most famous landmark along the Oregon Trail. It's located in western Nebraska.

cholera: A short-lasting, often fatal, disease caused by bacteria in dirty water, milk or food. Many overlanders died of cholera on the trip west.

chuck wagon: A wagon with a stove and provisions for cooking, as well as medicines and firewood.

claim: A section of public land staked out by a miner or homesteader.

Continental Divide: The high ground in the Rocky Mountains. On the east side the rivers flow toward the Mississippi River. On the west side the rivers flow toward the Pacific Ocean.

Corps of Discovery: Lewis and Clark's expedition into the Northwest. It was commissioned in 1804 by President Thomas Jefferson, who hoped Lewis and Clark would find a waterway to the Pacific.

corral: An enclosure formed by a circle of wagons, mainly to keep the livestock safe from coyotes.

cowboys: Someone on horseback who tended and drove herds of cattle, particularly in western United States and Canada.

Custer, George Armstrong: The American military leader best known for having died at the Battle of Little Bighorn (nicknamed Custer's Last Stand).

D

Deere, John: The designer of the first cast steel plow that would change the life of the prairie farmer.

delirium: Confusion and disorientation.

dime novel: Swift-moving, thrilling novels, mainly about the American Revolution, the frontier period, and the Civil War. The books were first sold in 1860 for 10 cents.

Donner Party: A wagon train that was trapped by early blizzards in the Sierra Nevada. Only 45 of the original 89 settlers survived.

drought: A long period without rain that can often cause extensive damage to crops.

Dutch oven: A heavy cast-iron pot with a tight-fitting lid that was used for baking as well as cooking.

dysentery: A painful, sometimes fatal disorder of the intestines, characterized by severe diarrhea.

E

emigrant: A person who leaves one country or region to settle in another. Before Oregon and California were officially part of the United States, pioneers were called emigrants.

F

Fort Laramie: A trading fort overlooking the Platte River in present-day Wyoming.

Forty-Niners: People who went to California in the rush for gold in 1849.

frontier: The boundary or edge of a settlement and civilization.

G

Great Migration: The first large wagon train to travel the length of the Oregon Trail.

H

homesteader: A person who settled and farmed land, especially under the Homestead Act.

husking bee: A bee that focused on husking corn.

I

immigrant: A person who moves to a new country to settle there permanently.

Independence Rock: A giant dome-like rock in southwestern Wyoming that thousands of emigrants carved their names into.

Indian Territory: An area designated by Congress in the 1830s. It stretched from Texas to the Missouri River in what is present-day Oklahoma. Native Americans from the East were forced from their homelands and sent to live in the Indian Territory. Later, most of this land became open to white homesteaders during the Oklahoma Land Rush of 1889.

Indian Wars: A series of conflicts between the United States and Native Americans.

Isthmus of Panama: The narrow strip of land that lies between the Caribbean Sea and the Pacific Ocean, linking North and South America

J

jumping-off places: Towns along the Missouri River that served as gathering spots for pioneer families who wanted to join a wagon train.

L

land speculators: People who made money by claiming prairie land and reselling it.
lard: A soft white solid fat from hogs.
lye: Ashes dissolved in water.

M

Manifest Destiny: The belief that the United States had a mission to expand across North America.
Mormon Trail: A trail that paralleled the Oregon Trail until Fort Bridger in modern-day Wyoming. The first Mormon emigrants made their way along this trail in 1846.
Mormons: A religious group. Many Mormons walked to the Great Salt Lake in Utah pushing handcarts with all their belongings in them during the Great Migration in the 1850s.
mountain men: Fur trappers who used their knowledge of the West to become explorers, scouts, and guides for wagon trains.

N

Native American: The people who lived in North and South America before Europeans arrived. They lived off the land and their cultures were routed in the natural world.

O

Oklahoma Land Rush: One day when nearly 2 million acres in the heart of Indian Territory were opened to homesteading in 1889. One hundred thousand people lined up, ready to stake a claim when the bugles blew at noon. By nightfall, all the acres in the Oklahoma District had been claimed.
Oregon Fever: An obsession with the idea of moving to the West.
Oregon Trail: A 2,100-mile trail that began at "jumping off places" in communities along the Missouri River and went through the Plains and the Rocky Mountains, until it ended in the Willamette Valley of western Oregon.
overlanders: Pioneers who made their way west by land (unlike those who went west by a sea route).
ox yoke: A wooden bar that links two oxen together. The oxen would then be attached to the wagon. There were no reins so oxen were guided by a pioneer walking beside them.
oxen: Large, strong animals that pulled wagons and plows for pioneers and farmers. Although they were slower than horses they could pull more.

P

panning: To wash earth and sand away from gold in a pan.

Parting of the Ways sites: places where emigrants left the Oregon Trail to turn south for California.
Pemmican: A traditional food eaten by Native Americans and adopted by the mountain men as they explored the frontier.
persecution: Harm or suffering inflicted on someone because they are different.
petroglyphs: Carvings on rock.
pictographs: Paintings on rock.
pilot bread or hardtack: A very hard biscuit made from flour and water. Hardtack was often taken on long journeys because it would keep for a long time.
pioneer: One of the first to settle in a territory.
Pony Express: A speedy mail delivery service in the West. It was made up of young men and fast horses who covered as much as 250 miles per day. This mail service lasted about 18 months until the telegraph put it out of business.
portraiture: The art of drawing or taking a picture of someone.
prairie schooners: A name given to covered wagons.
prairie: The wide, rolling land west of the Missouri-Mississippi Valley characterized by tall grasses and few trees.
Preemption Act: A law that granted settlers the right to purchase up to 160 acres of public land, provided they improved it by building a shelter on it and farming it for 12 months.
Promontory Summit: The place near Ogden, Utah, where the Central Pacific and the Union Pacific railroads connected in a grand ceremony in 1869, creating the first railroad line linking east to west.
prospector: Someone who explores an area for valuable natural resources, like gold.
puncheons: The flat side of logs cut in half the long way, often laid together for floors.

Q

quilting bee: A bee that consisted of only women and in which the focus of work was on making quilts.

R

remuda: The herd of extra horses for the cowboys.
reservations: Land set aside for Native Americans by the U.S. government. By 1883, virtually all Native American tribes had been confined to reservations where they were expected to abandon their own languages and cultures and adopt English and learn how to farm.
round up: To collect cattle by riding around them and driving them to move in together.

S

scurvy: A sometimes fatal disease people get when they don't have enough ascorbic acid in their diet. Symptoms include loose teeth, and bleeding, painful gums. Pioneers had problems with scurvy when crossing the west by wagon train.
secede: To quit, leave, or withdraw.
Shoshone: A Native American people of what is now the Western United States.
silhouette: An outline of somebody or something filled in with blackness or shadow.
skillet: A cast-iron frying pan.
slaughterhouse: The place where animals are butchered for market.
soddie: Temporary homes made of sod- or earth-bricks stacked together.
stampede: A sudden uncontrolled rush of a group of animals.
Strauss, Levi: A German immigrant who made his way to San Francisco with some cotton material called denim that he thought would be great for making tents. Instead he made pants. Today, we're still wearing "Levis."
Sutter's Mill: The site of the first gold strike in California in 1848 leading to the California Gold Rush.

T

tallow: Melted animal fat used for making candles and soap, as well as waterproofing things.
tarpaper: A heavy paper coated with tar, often used as a roof because it was relatively waterproof.
toll: A tax or fee paid for the right to pass through an area or over a road or bridge.
transcontinental railroad: A railroad that spans all or at least most of the continent. The first transcontinental railroad in the United States was completed in 1869, after track was laid over 1,700 miles (2,700 km) between Sacramento, California, and Omaha, Nebraska.
treaty: A formal agreement between two or more nations.
typhoid: A highly contagious and often fatal disease caused by bacteria. Symptoms were fever, diarrhea, headaches, and eventually hemorrhaging and confusion.

W

wagon train: A group of trains that traveled across the country in a line.
Wild West shows: A spectacular show organized in 1883 by William F. Cody, nicknamed Buffalo Bill. The show featured horseback riding and marksmanship demonstrations and exhibited the wild spirit of the West.

RESOURCES

Allen, John Logan. *Jedediah Smith and the Mountain Men of the American West*. Chelsea House, 1991.

Bial, Raymond. *Frontier Home*. Houghton Mifflin, 1993.

Broida, Marian. *Projects about Westward Expansion*. Benchmark Books, 2004.

Collier, Christopher. *Indians, Cowboys, and Farmers and the Battle for the Great Plains,* Benchmark Books, 2000.

Doherty, Kieran. *Voyageurs, Lumberjacks, and Farmers: Pioneers of the Midwest*. The Oliver Press, 2004.

_____ *Ranchers, Homesteaders, and Traders: Frontiersmen of the South-Central States*. The Oliver Press, 2001.

Duncan, Dayton. *People of the West*. The West Project, 1996.

Green, Carl R. *The Mission Trails in American History*. Enslow Publishers, 2001.

Greenwood, Barbara. *Pioneer Crafts*. Kids Can Press, 1997.

_____ *A Pioneer Sampler: The Daily Life of a Pioneer Family in 1840*. Houghton Mifflin, 1995.

Harvey, Brett. *Farmers and Ranchers*. 21st Century Books, 1995.

Herb, Angela M. *Beyond the Mississippi: Early Westward Expansion of the United States*. Lodestar Books, 1996.

Hevly, Nancy. *Preachers and Teachers*. 21st Century Books, 1995.

Josephson, Judith Pinkerton. *Growing up in Pioneer America, 1800–1890*. Lerner Publications Company, 2003.

King, David C. *Pioneer Days: Discover the Past with Fun Projects, Games, Activities, and Recipes*. John Wiley & Sons, Inc., 1997.

Markel, Rita J. *Your Travel Guide to America's Old West*. Lerner Publications Company, 2004.

Morley, Jacqueline. *You Wouldn't Want to be an American Pioneer*. Franklin Watts, 2002.

_____ *How Would you Survive in the American West?* Franklin Watts, 1995.

Reef, Catherine. *Buffalo Soldiers*. 21st Century Books, 1993.

Ritchie, David. *Frontier Life: Life in America 100 Years Ago*. Chelsea House Publishers, 1996.

Sandler, Martin W. *Pioneers: A Library of Congress Book*. Harper Collins, 1994.

Sigerman, Harriet. *Land of Many Hands; Women in the American West*. Oxford University Press, 1997.

Stefoff, Rebecca. *The Oregon Trail in American History*. Enslow Publishers Inc., 1997.

_____ *Women Pioneers*. Facts on File, 1995.

Stegner, Page. *Winning the Wild West: The Epic Saga of the American Frontier, 1800-1899*. The Free Press, 2002.

Sundling, Charles W. *Cowboys of the Frontier*. Abdo Publishing Company, 2000.

Uschan, Michael V. *Westward Expansion*. Lucent Books, 2001.

Wadsworth, Ginger. *Words West: Voices of Young Pioneers*. Clarion Books, 2003.

Weinstein, Allen and David Rubel. *The Story of America*. Agincourt Press, 2002.

INDEX